Christianity

ANNE GELDART

Heinemann

Heinemann Educational Publishers
Halley Court, Jordan Hill, Oxford OX2 8EJ
a division of Reed Educational & Professional Publishing Ltd

OXFORD MELBOURNE AUCKLAND
JOHANNESBURG BLANTYRE GABORONE
IBADAN PORTSMOUTH (NH) USA CHICAGO

Heinemann is a registered trademark of Reed Educational &
Professional Publishing Ltd

© Anne Geldart, 1999

First published in 2000

03 02 01 00
10 9 8 7 6 5 4 3 2 1

British Library Cataloguing in Publication Data
A catalogue record for this book is available from the British Library

Geldart, Anna
    Christianity – (Exploring religions)
    1. Christianity – Juvenile literature
    I. Title
    230

ISBN 0 431 09303 2. This title is also available in a hardback library
edition (ISBN 0 431 09302 4).

Designed and typeset by Gecko Ltd, Bicester, Oxon
Illustrated by Mike Parsons and Chris Rothero
Printed and bound in Spain by Edelvives

Acknowledgements

The author would like to thank Joe Jenkins for his valuable comments
on the manuscript of this book; Sue Walton, Jane Tyler, Robert Bircher
and the rest of the Heinemann team; and her husband, without whose
help and support this book would not have been written.

The publishers would like to thank the following for permission to
reproduce copyright material.
Amnesty International for the extracts on pp. 133 and 147, reproduced
by permission of Amnesty International British Section, 99 Rosebery
Avenue, London EC1R 4RE; British Yearly Meeting of the Religious
Society of Friends for extracts from *Quaker Faith and Practice*, 1995, by
Meg Maslin and Pat Saunders, on pp. 135, 155; CARE (Christian Action
Research and Education) for the quotation by Anna Grear on p. 137;
Cassell plc for the extracts from *The Catechism of the Catholic Church*,
published by Geoffrey Chapman, 1994, on pp. 48, 126; the Catholic
Media Office for the extract from *All People Together* on p. 140; the
extract from *The Alternative Service Book 1980* is copyright © The
Central Board of Finance of the Church of England 1980, The
Archbishops' Council 1999 and is reproduced by permission on p. 91,
the extract from an unpublished paper by the Board for Social
responsibility of the Church of England, 1990, is copyright © The Central
Board of Finance of the Church of England 1990, The Archbishops'
Council 1999 and is reproduced by permission on p. 142, the extract
from the Board for Social responsibility of the Church of England,
*Human Fertilisation and Embryology. The Response of the Board for
Social Responsibility to the DHSS Report of the Committee of Inquiry*
(November 1984) is copyright © The Central Board of Finance of the
Church of England 1984, The Archbishops' Council 1999 and is
reproduced by permission on p. 145; The Christian Education Movement

for the extract from *Ecumenical Movement*, by Dr Lorna Brockett, on
p. 47; Church in Wales Publications for extracts from © 1993 Holy
Matrimony and © 1993 The Order for the Burial of the Dead, on pp. 1
123; Darton, Longman & Todd for the extract taken from *The Capacity
Love*, by Jack Dominian, published and copyright 1985 by Darton,
Longman and Todd Ltd, and used by permission of the publishers on
p. 121; the Estate of Martin Luther King, Jr. for the quotations on pp. 5,
32, 35, 38, 128, 131, reprinted by arrangement with The Heirs to the
Estate of Martin Luther King, Jr., c/o Writers House, Inc. as agent for th
proprietor; Faber and Faber for the extract from *The Last Temptation*,
1975, by Nikos Kazantzakis, reproduced by permission of the publisher
on p. 27; Matthew Fox for the extracts from *The Coming of the Cosmic
Christ*, published by HarperCollins Inc., San Francisco, 1988, and
Original Blessing, published by Bear & Company, Santa Fe, on pp. 5, 1C
106, 129, 154; HarperCollins Publishers for the extract from *Hope and
Suffering*, by Desmond Tutu, on p. 78; Hodder and Stoughton for the
extracts from *Revelations of Divine Love*, by Halcyon Backhouse, on
pp. 33, 99, 125, reproduced by permission of Hodder and Stoughton
Limited; Methodist Publishing House for extracts from *Methodist
Conference Statements* 1990 and 1991, © Trustees for Methodist Churc
Purposes, used by permission of Methodist Publishing House on pp.
115, 129, 145; National Council for Gibran for the extracts from poetry
Kahil Gibran on pp. 39, 125; Henri Nouwen for the quotation on p. 107
the Office for National Statistics for the statistics on pp. 119, 148; the
Orion Publishing Group Ltd for the extract from *Gnostic Gospels*, by
Elaine Pagels, reproduced by permission of the publishers Weidenfeld
and Nicolson, on p.43; Penguin Books Ltd for the extracts from
Belonging to the Universe, by Fritjof Capra, on pp. 41, 153, and *A New
Model of the Universe*, by Peter Ouspensky, on p. 83; Dr Melissa
Raphael, Religious Studies Department, Cheltenham and Gloucester
College of Higher Education, for the quotations on pp. 70–1; Resurgenc
for the quotation by Brother David, originally published in *Resurgence
Magazine*, on p. 75; Routledge for the extract from *Waiting for God*, by
Simone Weil, translated by Emma Cranford, on p. 30; The Salvation
Army for the quotation on p. 130; George Sassoon for 'Everyone Sang',
by Siegfried Sassoon, on p. 77; Suhrkamp Verlag for *If the War Goes On*
by Herman Hesse, on p. 67; Trust of Religious Education for the extract
from *Christianity and the World Religions*, 1987, by Hans Küng, on
p. 47; Father Gregory Wirdnam for the quotation on pp. 50–1; John Woo
for the extract on p. 112; the World Council of Churches for the extracts
from *One World* magazine on pp. 56, 57. Unless otherwise
acknowledged, scriptures quoted throughout this book are from the
Good News Bible published by The Bible Societies/HarperCollins
Publishers Ltd., UK, © American Bible Society, 1966, 1971, 1976, 1992.

The publishers would like to thank the following for permission to
reproduce photographs.
Art Gallery of Western Australia, Perth/Bridgeman Art Library p. 96; Va
Baker/Andes Press Agency p. 72; Bridgeman Art Library pp. 16, 18, 23
25, 26, 28, 39, 71, 82, 100, 109; British Museum/Bridgeman Art Librar
p. 13; Camera Press p. 35 (right); J. Allen Cash p. 58; Werner
Dieterich/Image Bank p. 22; S.K. Dutt/Camera Press p. 35 (left);
Glasgow Museums p. 99; Robin Hanbury-Tenison/Survival
International p. 128; David Hoffman p. 134; Hutchinson Library
pp. 11, 57, 80 (left), 83 (Tony Souter), 110 (Patricia Goycoolea); Keble
College, Oxford/Bridgeman Art Library p. 6; Keith Ellis Collection
pp. 54, 84, 98; Lightmotif-Paoluzzo p. 66; Murdo MacLeod p. 126;
Danny McKenzie at New Generation Art p. 7; Magnum Photos pp. 68
(S. Meiselas), 90 (Henri Cartier-Bresson), 146, 150 (H. Gruyaert), 154
(Sebastio Salgado); Museum of Modern Art, New York/Bridgeman Art
Library p. 32; National Gallery p. 74; Network pp. 60 (Paul Lowe), 64
(Tony Pupkewitz/Rapho), 78 (Mike Goldwater), 149 (Jenny Matthews);
Bury Peerless p. 104; Popperfoto p. 35 (centre), 62; Carlos
Reyes/Andes Press Agency pp. 103, 106; Carlos Reyes-Manzo/Andes
Press Agency pp. 65, 80 (right), 108, 113; Science Photo Library pp. 5
(Tony Hallas), 143 (Hank Morgan); Estate of Stanley Spencer for 'The
Scorpion' by Stanley Spencer, © Estate of Stanley Spencer All rights
reserved, DACS 1999, p. 96; Tate Gallery p. 30 (John Webb); The de
Morgan Foundation/Bridgeman Art Library p. 122; The Society of
Friends p. 86; Mark Wadlow/Russia & Republics Photo Library p. 50.
Cover photograph by Hutchinson Library.

The publishers have made every effort to contact copyright holders.
However, if any material has been incorrectly acknowledged, the
publishers would be pleased to correct this at the earliest opportunity

CONTENTS

SA013232

From the earliest times, humans have had moments when they were struck by a sense of **awe**. They feel wonder, excitement or even a kind of fear. It may be caused by the power of a volcano as it erupts, or the vastness of the ocean. The new growth of plants every spring might seem wonderful after the snows of winter. The births of their own children are moments of great joy.

Some people think that the feeling of awe is the beginning of religion. This is the time when people start to realize that there is more to life than what we can see, hear, taste or touch. People have believed, and still believe, that as well as the outer world that we can see, there is an inner, invisible, spiritual world.

Throughout history, there have been many great teachers who have helped people to understand about their place in the world. Even now, they still help people to answer some basic questions such as:

- How and why did the universe come into being?

- How and why am I here?

- What is life all about?

These teachers include Abraham, Moses, Confucius, the Buddha, Jesus Christ, Muhammad and Guru Nanak. They helped to found the great world religions of Judaism, Confucianism, Buddhism, Christianity, Islam and Sikhism. These religions have helped millions of people to find a purpose in life.

THE SEARCH

Although the Western world is less religious than it used to be, people still ask basic questions about life. They still want to know whether there is something more to life than just existing. Religions help people to explore their thoughts and feelings about what is important in life.

THIS BOOK

This book is about the Christian religion. There are over a thousand million Christians in the world. Christianity is an important part of the culture of many nations.

Many other religions are followed by millions of people in countries all over the world, including Britain. This brings about a multi-faith society, where we can share a wide variety of music, literature, food, dress, beliefs and customs.

Religion has two parts: the outward, visible part and the inward part. The outward part includes the actions of religion, for example, reading holy books, praying, going to worship, wearing special clothes or eating special food. The inward part is about the meaning that believers give to their actions. It is concerned with belief, intention and feelings.

This book describes the outward aspects of Christianity and the **faith** and intentions of Christian believers.

This book is meant to help you to think for yourself about your own life and things that are, or will become, important to you. It will help you to understand Christian beliefs about life.

Words in **bold print** are explained in the Glossary on pages 157–8.

REFLECTIONS

When I see the glories of the cosmos, I can't help but believe that there is a Divine Hand behind it all.

(Albert Einstein, 1879–1955 – scientist)

Nature is the art of God.

(Teilhard de Chardin, 1881–1955 – scientist and priest)

'... the great things in this universe are things that we never see. You walk out at night and look up at the beautiful stars as they bedeck the heavens like swinging lanterns of eternity, and you think you can see all. Oh, no. You can never see the law of gravitation that holds them there.'

(Dr Martin Luther King, 1929–69)

Sean's story

We took a group of Year 11 pupils from the city for a study weekend in West Wales. Some of them wanted to go for a walk beside the sea. It was March, the wind was gusting strongly across the Irish Sea onto the deserted beach. The sun was brilliant. I saw Sean standing on top of a rocky outcrop, arms stretched out as though to embrace the empty blue sky, his anorak ballooning round his body. He was making a keening, wordless sound, 'Aaaah! Aaaah!' He turned to me, 'Miss, I never felt like this before.' He gulped, tears streaming down his wind-reddened face. 'It's...it's – magic!'

(Sean's tutor)

POINTS OF VIEW

- Though we are God's sons and daughters we do not realize it yet.

  (Meister Eckhart *c.*1260–1328 – monk and mystic)

- I may have in myself the secret and meaning of the earth, the golden sun, the light, the foam-flecked sea.

  (Richard Jefferies 1848–87 – Wiltshire writer)

- The universe loves us every day the sun rises, and the creator loves us through creation.

  (Matthew Fox – priest, theologian and educator)

LOVE AND...

- There is no love without hope, no hope without love, and neither hope nor love without faith.

  (St Augustine of Hippo – early Christian thinker)

INTRODUCTION

This section is a brief account of the most important parts of the life of Jesus **Christ**. If you want to know more about him, read one of the **Gospels** of Matthew, Mark, Luke and John. These are the first four books of the New Testament.

JESUS CHRIST

Jesus Christ means 'Jesus the **Messiah**'. Christ is a Greek word and Messiah is Hebrew. Both words mean 'the anointed one'. To anoint someone means to pour special oil, that has been blessed, on them.

Background

Jesus was born in Bethlehem in Judea in about 4 BCE. He was brought up in Galilee in the north. His mother's name was Mary. Jesus was Jewish. At that time the Romans ruled that part of the world. Most Jews hated this. They longed for God to send a warrior king, who would defeat the Romans and set the Jewish people free. The man would be the Messiah, God's chosen one. Some Jews thought that when he came, there would be a final battle and afterwards God would make everything new again. Some Jews, known as Zealots, became freedom-fighters. Others went to live in the desert to pray while they waited for the Messiah to come.

Jesus' life as a teacher

One holy man who lived in the desert was called John the Baptist. He **baptized** people to prepare for the coming of the Messiah. He dipped people in the river as a sign of washing away **sins**. He baptized Jesus in the River Jordan.

> As soon as Jesus came up out of the water, he saw heaven opening and the Spirit coming down on him like a dove. And a voice came from heaven, 'You are my own dear Son. I am pleased with you.'
>
> (Mark 1:10–11)

After this, Jesus collected twelve **disciples** or followers. He went about preaching, teaching and healing the sick and mentally ill. It was even said that he brought people back to life and performed miracles. He spoke out against injustice and taught people about love, forgiveness and peace. Crowds soon came to hear and see Jesus, but the rulers of the country were not pleased with him. They thought Jesus kept company with the wrong kind of people. He was not the sort of Messiah they expected.

Finally, Jesus was arrested and tried in Jerusalem. He was **crucified** (nailed on a cross) and died. However, all the Gospels report that on the third day Jesus rose from the dead.

An artist's impression of Jesus 'The Light of the World'

Christians call this the **Resurrection** (see units 5, 7 and 49). The followers of Jesus saw him alive after this. They also saw his **ascension**, when he went up into heaven (see unit 51).

DID JESUS EXIST?

Most Christians believe that the Gospels are a good guide to the life, death and teachings of Jesus. Some scholars are not so sure. They think the writers were influenced by the **Church** to write what they did, and not by Jesus. However, the Gospels were written about 30 to 80 years after the death of Jesus, so most of what is in them is accurate.

Other writers also give evidence that shows Jesus did exist. In the first century, Tacitus (a Roman) and Josephus (a Jewish historian) mention Jesus and the early Christians. In the second century the Roman writers Pliny and Seutonius also refer to Jesus.

BASIC CHRISTIAN IDEAS ABOUT JESUS

All Christians believe that Jesus actually lived on earth as described in the Gospels. They also believe that:

- Jesus was a great teacher, who gave an example to others. He taught that a person must be *pure in heart*. It is not good enough to *pretend* to be a good person.

- Jesus showed through his life, death and resurrection just how much God loves the world. Christians believe that 'God loved the

An artist's impression of Jesus on the cross

world so much that he sent his only Son, so that everyone who believes in him may not die but have eternal life.' (John 3:16).

- Jesus is as alive today as he was when he lived on the earth 2000 years ago. Christians feel him as a living presence in their lives.

- God became human when Jesus was born. This is called the **incarnation**. Christians see this as an act of love, but also an act of **salvation**. By becoming human, God made it possible for people to return to him. Jesus Christ showed what God is really like.

POINTS OF VIEW

Jesus of Nazareth was a man whose divine authority was clearly proven to you by all the miracles and wonders which God performed through him.

(Peter's sermon in Acts 2:22)

FACTFILE

Definition
Gospel: the good news of salvation through Jesus Christ

INTRODUCTION

The **Bible** is the Christian holy book. Its name comes from a Greek word *biblia*, which means 'the books'. It is also called **scripture**, or the scriptures. The Bible is not one book, but a whole library of books.

It took about a thousand years for the Bible to be completed. The last book was written in about 90 CE.

The two main sections of the Bible are the Old Testament and the New Testament. They are called testaments (agreements) because Christians believe that God made a special agreement with human beings. These promises are also called God's covenant.

The Old Testament contains 39 books. These are also the Jewish scriptures. They were mostly written in Hebrew, with a few sections in Aramaic. In about 300 BCE, 70 holy men translated the Hebrew scriptures into Greek. This Greek translation was called the Septuagint. In the next 200 years another group of books called the **Apocrypha** (a Greek word meaning 'hidden things') was introduced. The early Christians used these two groups of writings. Later, some Christians rejected the Apocrypha.

In the first century CE, Christians wrote another 27 books. They became known as the New Testament. They are about Jesus and his followers. The New Testament was written in Greek. This was the most commonly used language of the Roman Empire at the time of Jesus.

So the Christian Bible is a library of 66 books. If you include the Apocrypha, there are 79 books.

THE OLD TESTAMENT – THE JEWISH SCRIPTURES

The Old Testament is important to both Jews and Christians. The New Testament writers often quote from the Old Testament to show that the Jewish Scriptures prophesy (fore-tell) that Jesus would come.

In English translation, the 39 Old Testament books include:
  5 law books
  12 history books
  5 poetry books
  17 books of prophecy

THE NEW TESTAMENT

The New Testament contains:
  5 history books
  21 letters of the early Church, sometimes called '**epistles**'
  1 book of prophecy – the *Book of Revelation*

Four of the history books are the Gospels (a word meaning 'Good News'). These tell the

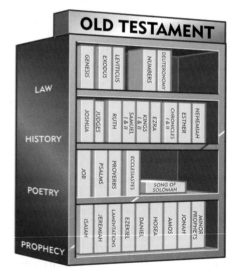

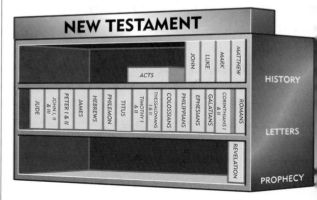

The books that make up the Bible

tory of the life and teaching of Jesus. The Gospels are called *Matthew, Mark, Luke* and *John* after the men who may have written them. The first three are called the Synoptic Gospels. They are similar in style and use similar stories and events. Most experts think they may have been written between 60 and 110 CE, with Mark's Gospel being the first. John's Gospel is different in style from the others, and may have been written at a later time.

The fifth history book is the *Acts of the Apostles*. It is about the early days of the Church and concentrates on the lives of Peter, one of Jesus' close friends, and Paul, an early Christian missionary.

Early Christian leaders wrote the 21 letters (or epistles). These men wrote to the new Churches giving advice and guidance.

The prophetic book is the *Book of Revelation*. It is sometimes called the **Apocalypse**. It is full of visions, symbols and strange events. Its theme is that good will win over evil, and that Christ will one day return to earth in victory.

HOW THE BIBLE CAME TO US

John Wycliffe translated the Bible into English in the fourteenth century. The first approved translation in English was the 'Great Bible' of 1539. Before this, Bibles in Britain were written in Latin. There are now many translations of the Bible in modern English to make it easier to understand.

THE BIBLE IN CHRISTIAN LIFE AND WORSHIP

All Scripture is inspired by God, and is useful for teaching the truth, rebuking error, correcting faults and giving instruction for right living.

(2 Timothy, 3:16, *Good News Bible*)

Christians believe that the Bible is in some way the Word of God. It can teach, inspire and guide them in their everyday lives.

In Christian worship, parts of the Bible (called lessons) are read aloud while the **congregation** (the people in church) listens. Usually there is a lesson from the Old Testament or the Apocrypha and one from the New Testament. One of the Psalms may be recited or sung.

Christians also study the Bible at home, in small groups or alone. They believe the Bible can help them understand their faith better.

FACTFILE

Translating the Bible

Many Christians died so that the Bible could be written in a language everyone can understand. William Tyndale (c.1494–1536) could not persuade the Church to support his work of translating the Bible into English. He was hounded out of England and had to finish the task in Germany. He worked from original Hebrew and Greek manuscripts. His first New Testament translation was printed in 1525. His books had to be smuggled into England. His enemies said he was a heretic, which meant that his beliefs were wrong. He was executed by being strangled and burned at the stake in 1536.

This unit looks at some key questions about what the Bible means for Christians.

Key question 1 *How can Christians believe in a collection of books as old as the Bible?*

People may ask, 'Is the Bible true? How do we know that it wasn't just made up?' Christians may answer in a number of ways.

First, each of the world religions has its own **sacred** scriptures (holy books). These scriptures appeared at various times and in different parts of the world, but they all share basic themes. They all teach that the world and the universe did not just happen. They were created by a great power and they have a purpose. Humans also have a purpose. They have a divine spark, something god-like, in them and they are part of the great plan for the universe. The Bible and other sacred writings help to explain this purpose.

Second, many of the places and events we read about in the Bible appear in other historical evidence. Non-Christian writers from the time of Jesus, such as Tacitus and Josephus, also tell of Jesus. The Bible is one of the world's oldest collections of books. We do not reject other historical records, so we should not reject the Bible either.

Third, many of the writings in the Bible are wise teachings about how human beings should treat each other and the world they live in. These teachings are as true today as they were 2000 years ago, because human nature doesn't change.

Key question 2 *What does it mean to say the Bible is the Word of God?*

Christians use other books for worship and study, as well as the Bible, but the Bible is special. It has authority. Christians believe God speaks to them through the Bible. However, the expression 'the Word of God' means different things to different Christians.

- **Fundamentalist** Christians believe the Bible does not contain human words, but God's words. It cannot be wrong. They think the Bible is the actual word of God passed down by the writers. For them the Bible is true in every word, since it is literally the Word of God.

- Conservative Christians believe the Word of God came directly to the writers, but that their own thoughts and opinions affected what they wrote. For these Christians the Bible is the Word of God, interpreted by the human mind.

- Liberal Christians believe that some holy people had special gifts of insight. They had special understanding of the working of the human mind that others did not have, and could put this into words. These writers were inspired by God, but they were human so sometimes they made mistakes. So the Bible contains the Word of God, but it is not literally the Word of God.

- Finally, there is the view that the Bible is a faith document. It is not a history book or a science book, but a book about what it truly means to be human. It can be read literally, but it has deeper meaning about our human nature as it is, and how we may change and grow.

This shows how Christians may differ about what the Bible means. For instance, fundamentalist Christians believe that God made the world in six days. They reject the Theory of Evolution. Conservative Christians see the six-day creation story as a poem which says why the world was made, not how. Liberal Christians and others see the account as a symbolic story which tries to explain the mystery of creation (see unit 6).

Christians believe that the Bible has meaning today

Key question 3 *How can a book that is 2000 years old have any meaning for people today*

The writers of the Bible knew nothing about nuclear weapons, test-tube babies or pollution. However, human nature does not change. The basic teachings about human behaviour last for ever. These teachings about love, mercy,forgiveness, justice and kindness are as useful today as they were 2000 years ago.

Key question 4 *How much authority does the Bible have among Christians?*

Authority, in this sense, means something that should be accepted, obeyed or respected. Christians believe that the basis for their beliefs and practices comes from three sources: the Bible; the Church and people's own consciences or feelings.

If Christians need help with a particular problem, they may find help from any or all of these sources. For example, some Roman Catholics (see unit 23) think the Church should decide what the Bible means. For them, the authority of the Church is greater than the authority of the Bible.

Many Protestants (see unit 25) believe that final authority comes from the Bible, rather than the Church.

FACTFILE

The Church at Corinth

Two of St Paul's letters in the New Testament are addressed to 'the Church of God which is at Corinth'. The Church had about 30–40 members who met in a room in a private house. Corinth was a city with 200,000 citizens and 500,000 slaves. It was the most sinful city in the ancient world. The temple of Aphrodite had over 1000 'sacred prostitutes'. There were always lots of sailors who were just passing through – with three months pay and nothing much to do, except drink and womanize. Yet here St Paul established one of the first Christian Churches among the gentiles, 'The Church of God among the Godless'! The Christian Church did not have an easy beginning.

POINTS OF VIEW

Happy is the man who becomes wise – who gains understanding. There is more profit in it than there is in silver; it is worth more to you than gold. Wisdom is more valuable than jewels; nothing you could want can compare with it.

(Proverbs 3:13–15)

THE APOSTLES' CREED

I believe in God the Father Almighty,
maker of Heaven and earth:
and in Jesus Christ his only Son our
    Lord,
who was conceived by the Holy Ghost,
born of the Virgin Mary,
suffered under Pontius Pilate,
was crucified, dead and buried.
He descended into hell.
The third day he rose again from the
    dead;
he ascended into heaven,
and is seated at the right hand of God
the Father Almighty;
from thence he shall come to judge the
    quick and the dead.
I believe in the Holy Ghost;
the Holy Catholic Church;
the communion of saints;
the forgiveness of sins;
the resurrection of the body;
and the life everlasting. **AMEN**.

('ghost' here means 'spirit'.)

Creed means 'belief'. The Apostles' Creed was written around 450 CE. It lists some of the central beliefs of the Christian religion.

This unit looks at some of the main ideas about God, the **Holy Spirit** and Jesus. Later, we shall examine these beliefs in more depth.

GOD

Christians believe in a God who is Father, Son and Holy Spirit. These are not separate gods, but different aspects of the same God. Christians use the idea of the **Trinity** (see unit 8) to explain this.

In the thirteenth century, an unknown English writer wrote a book called *The Cloud of Unknowing* about the mystery of God.

He may well be loved, but He may not be thought of. He may be reached and held close by means of love, but by means of thought, never.

(The Cloud of Unknowing)

The writer means that, however much people try to know God with their minds, they only really know God through their deepest emotions.

However, some characteristics of God are thought to be: God is One, the creator, omnipotent (all powerful), omnipresent (present everywhere), omniscient (all-knowing), benevolent (kind), holy, perfect, a personal God.

THE HOLY SPIRIT

Christians believe the Holy Spirit is a power that gives them guidance and inner strength. The Holy Spirit gives people special gifts. It enables people to understand God, it helps people to be holy and show great love. The Holy Spirit is living and active through all human beings.

JESUS CHRIST

Although the different Churches may disagree about the details of Christian belief and forms of worship (see units 23, 24, 25) all the main Churches agree that Jesus Christ represents God's presence on earth.

These beliefs in the incarnation (see unit 2) are expressed in worship. They have also affected theology (the study of religion), religious practices, everyday life and belief.

Jesus has been described as 'all things to all people'. To a tradesman, he is a master craftsman. A soldier may see Jesus as the commander of his regiment who expects his total loyalty and courage. A nun may see Jesus as her spiritual husband.

Jesus' preaching, teaching and healing have inspired artists and poets, as well as ordinary people. The New Testament shows Jesus as completely human, yet at the same time divine (like God).

Jesus' death and resurrection are very important to Christian faith. Christians believe that God allowed his Son to die for human beings, to show how much he loves them.

Christians believe that by rising from death, Jesus has prepared the way for human beings to have eternal (lasting for ever) life. The resurrection is a mystery, and is at the very heart of the Christian faith.

THE IMAGE OF GOD

Christ is the visible likeness of the invisible God. He is the first-born Son, superior to all created things. For through him God created everything in heaven and on earth, the seen and the unseen things, including spiritual powers, lords, rulers, and authorities. God created the whole universe through him and for him. Christ existed before all things. … God made peace through his Son's death on the cross and so brought back to himself all things, both on earth and in heaven.

(Colossians 1:15–17 and 19–20)

FACTFILE

Why have creeds?

Why do Christians have creeds? At first, the main reason was so that people who became members of the Church knew what the Church believed in and what they were committing themselves to. Creeds were statements that every new member had to make immediately before being baptized. Later, there were arguments within the Church when outsiders tried to join the Church and change its beliefs. These events made it necessary to agree on a statement that all Christians would accept. The two Creeds regularly used by Christians today are the Apostles' Creed (opposite) and the Nicene Creed.

Christians believe that Jesus' death shows how great the love of God is

SPIRIT

God is spirit

Not many Christians believe in the simple idea of God as a wise, kind old man with a long white beard, sitting on a golden throne somewhere up beyond the clouds.

In John's Gospel, Jesus says, 'God is spirit' (John 4:24). Spirit is different from the human form. It is more like a powerful force, or energy. Christians believe they can get in touch with this force through deep prayer and worship.

Other names for God might be Holy One, Ultimate Being, The Absolute. Whatever name is given to God, all Christians agree that the Power that created everything is a mystery.

CREATOR

Modern scientists and religious thinkers agree that it makes more sense to believe that the Universe was created, than that it just happened. This means there must be a creator.

In the past, some people thought that God actually made everything in six days. Some fundamentalist Christians (see unit 4) still believe this. Most other Christians believe the biblical account is symbolic. It points to the mysterious power of the Holy One. They argue that the wonders and beauty of nature, and the complex structures of life, down to the smallest atom, suggest order and planning. The planets, stars and suns also point towards a universe that is planned and has meaning.

Christians and many scientists reject the idea of a series of strange accidents or coincidences. Instead they argue that everything that exists came about through a creative power.

THE GROUND OF OUR BEING

Theologians are people who study ideas about God. Paul Tillich (1886–1965) used the phrase 'the ground of our being' to describe God. By this he meant that God is not 'a Being', but the basis of all life and existence. Humans live and die. We are finite. This means we have limits. But God has no limits. God has no beginning and no end and is therefore infinite. Because of this, our finite minds cannot fully understand the infinite mind (the source or ground of being). God is a mystery.

POINTS OF VIEW

- God is creating the entire universe fully and totally in this present now.

- Everything God created six thousand years ago – and even previous to that as God made the world – God creates now all at once. Everything which God created millions of years ago and everything which will be created by God after millions of years – if the world endures till then – God is creating all that in the innermost and deepest realms of the soul.

- Everything of the past and everything of the present and everything of the future God creates in the innermost realms of the soul.

(Meister Eckhart)

FACTFILE

The attributes of God

(An attribute is a feature or quality.)

- God is **omnipotent** – all powerful. God creates and controls all that exists.

- God is **omniscient** – all knowing. Nothing can be hidden from God.

- God is **transcendent** – beyond, outside the world's limits of time and space.

- God is **immanent** – within. God is present everywhere within the universe.

- God is **personal** – every human being can have a relationship with God on a personal level.

REFLECTIONS

The world and all that is in it belong
   to the Lord;
the earth and all who live on it
   are his.
He built it on the deep waters
   beneath the earth
and laid its foundations in the
   ocean depths.

(Psalm 24:1–2)

So God created human beings, making them to be like himself. He created them male and female…

(Genesis 1:27)

God is beauty.

(St Francis of Assisi, 1181–1225)

God is love.

(1 John 4:16)

Thomas Traherne, c.1636–74, a clergyman and poet, wrote about the way that pigs eat acorns but don't even think about the sun that gave them life. Nor do they think about the weather that made them grow or the tree from which they fell.

Jan van Ruysbroek, 1293–1381, founded a group of Christians who lived a life of prayer and meditation in a forest. He said, 'The image of God is found … in all humankind. Each possesses it whole, entire and undivided.' He was trying to explain that the image of God is expressed through the whole human race. 'In this way we are all one.'

The Apostles' Creed (see unit 5) says, 'I believe in Jesus Christ, his only Son, our Lord.' What do Christians mean when they say that Jesus is God's son?

THE SON OF GOD

As we saw in unit 6, God is spirit or creative power, not an old man with a white beard! The word 'son' is also used in a different way. Exactly who Jesus Christ was and what he was like is a deep mystery. The idea that he is God's 'only son' is a way of saying that Jesus was a person, full of holiness and goodness, who showed God's love to the world.

The New Testament has a number of ways of helping Christians to understand what 'the son of God' means.

In John 10:30 Jesus says, 'I and my Father are One,' and in Matthew 11:27, 'No one knows the Son except the Father, and no one knows the Father except the Son.' This suggests that Jesus was aware that in him – in his actions and suffering – God's work was being done.

In Philippians 2:6–8, it says:

> He always had the nature of God, but he did not think that by force he should try to become equal with God. Instead of this … he gave up all he had and took the nature of a servant. He became like a man. He was humble and walked the path of obedience all the way to death – his death on the cross.

The main ideas here are that God 'gave up all he had', 'took the nature of a servant', 'was humble' and was obedient 'all the way to death'. The key words are obedience, suffering and self-sacrifice. All this seems to say that God came down into the world, in human form, prepared to sacrifice himself, for the sake of his creation. And this is what being the son of God is all about.

The early Christian missionary, Paul, wrote about the idea of reconciliation (restoring friendship). He said that God sent his son so that humans could become adopted children of God. Reconciliation means that when they

Christians believe Jesus Christ was God in human form

are God's children, human beings can be free. People will no longer be slaves, held back by the burden of sin and guilt.

THE LORDSHIP OF JESUS

Another key phrase in the Apostles' Creed is 'Our Lord'. Lord is used in both the Old and New Testaments. This does not mean the same as an earthly ruler, with power or an army. For Christians, the true Lord is Jesus Christ, the man from Nazareth, who came to love and serve humanity. Christians believe not in the love of power, but in the power of love!

Christians believe that God became flesh and blood – truly human – in Jesus. In some mysterious way, God and humankind were joined together in the life of Jesus.

THE CROSS

The crucifixion (death on a cross) and resurrection of Jesus are basic Christian beliefs. The cross is a powerful symbol in the Christian religion. Christians have different thoughts about the cross.

First, the cross stands for a brutal and cruel death. God, in Jesus, suffered and died. He did this to show that good is stronger than evil, light more powerful than darkness.

Second, the cross shows that God cares about the struggles of everyday life. He gets involved.

Third, God wanted to show people the way forward. People could have chosen to listen to Jesus, but they didn't listen and nailed him to a cross.

Fourth, the cross represents the meeting point of 'ordinary time' with 'eternal time'. This is the here and now. This is something that helps in prayer and meditation.

Other views see Jesus' death on the cross as a sacrifice. By shedding his blood through Christ, God forgave and purified the human race. This is known as **atonement** – making up for past sins.

POINTS OF VIEW

The divine person who assumed our nature suffered death on the cross, a death which shook the earth, opened heaven and pleased God. From the first day of creation to the last night there has never been, nor will there be, so exalted and magnificent an act.

(Dante, 1265–1321 – Italian poet)

FACTFILE

Dietrich Bonhoeffer, 1906–45

Dietrich Bonhoeffer (see unit 74) followed Christ's example. He was hanged in Flossenburg concentration camp in April 1945. In his book, *The Cost of Discipleship*, Bonhoeffer wrote:

'When Christ calls to a man, He bids him come and die. It may be a death like that of the first disciples who had to leave home and work to follow him, or it may be a death like Luther's, who had to leave the monastery and go out into the world. But it is the same death every time...'

He was saying that sometimes Christians may have to die physically, but they all have to 'die' as far as their past life is concerned in order to start a new life with Christ.

8 THE TRINITY

INTRODUCTION

In the fifth century, St Patrick tried to explain Christian belief to the first people to join the Church in Ireland. He showed them a shamrock. Its leaf has three parts. The three parts make up the whole leaf. This is how St Patrick tried to explain the Trinity. Belief in the Trinity is very important to Christians. They use the Trinity to explain the relationship between God, Jesus Christ and the Holy Spirit.

WHAT IS THE TRINITY?

Christians speak of God as Father, Son and Holy Spirit. This is called the Trinity. 'Tri-' means three, and 'Unity' means one. So Trinity means three-in-one. It is rather like a triangle – three sides but one shape.

The Bible does not use the word 'Trinity', but there are verses that show the three-in-one in action. Mark's Gospel describes the baptism of Jesus like this:

> As soon as Jesus came up out of the water, he saw heaven opening and the Spirit coming down on him like a dove. And a voice came from heaven, 'You are my own dear Son. I am pleased with you.'
>
> (Mark 1:10–11)

Matthew's Gospel finishes with Jesus saying to his disciples:

> Go, then, to people everywhere and make them my disciples: baptize them in the name of the Father, the Son and the Holy Spirit.
>
> (Matthew 28:19–20)

In one of his letters to the Church at Corinth, Paul ends with a blessing, still used today, known as the Grace.

Christians speak of God as Father, Son and Holy Spirit

> The grace of the Lord Jesus Christ, the love of God, and the fellowship of the Holy Spirit be with you all.
>
> (2 Corinthians 13:13)

Verses like these helped the leaders of the early Church to work out the creeds (statements of Christian belief). They said that although the three parts of the Trinity work in different ways, they are all working together.

- God the Father is the Creator. He is the creative force behind the universe.

- The Son is God, born in human form (incarnated) as Jesus Christ. He is the Saviour working to **redeem** (save) the world.

- The Holy Spirit is the presence of God living within the world. The Spirit **sanctifies** – makes holy – and gives people new life.

These three, the Creator, **Redeemer** and Sanctifier, are not three gods, but one God working in three ways. It is important to know that the Christian religion is **monotheistic** – Christians believe in only one God.

The idea of the Trinity is monotheistic, too. Perhaps it is easier to think of God as having three roles, rather than being three separate people. In other words, God has three ways of being God.

The doctrine (teaching) of the Trinity sums up the Gospel, for some Christians. The words Father, Son and Holy Spirit refer to one and the same God. Christians cannot think or talk about God without referring to Jesus Christ and to the Holy Spirit. You can read more about the Trinity in unit 51.

THE HOLY SPIRIT

The Holy Spirit

In the Hebrew of the Old Testament, one word used for spirit is *ruah*. This means 'breath'. It is used to mean the life-giving breath of God. Another Hebrew word used is *lebab*. This means 'self' in the sense of self-awareness.

Who is the Holy Spirit? For Christians the Holy Spirit is a mystery who represents the love of God working in the world.

Christians believe that when Jesus speaks about being born again, he means a person allowing the Holy Spirit to enter their heart. When the Holy Spirit enters a human being it brings freedom, faith, goodness, joy and peace. It brings new life. It is part of God's creative power which continues to work in the world, among people.

Jesus refers to the Holy Spirit as the *paraclete* (in the Greek). This can be translated as 'helper', 'comforter' or 'advocate'.

FOOTPRINTS OF THE TRINITY

In the fourth century, St Augustine said there were traces of God, in the three forms of the Trinity, in everyday life. He called these traces 'footprints of the Trinity'. One example was the way that in human relationships the lover and the beloved were held together by their mutual love. Another was the way the human mind works. We have memory, reason and will-power – these are all activities of the mind which cannot be separated from each other.

FACTFILE

Christopher Columbus, 1451–1506, explorer

Christopher Columbus prayed to the Trinity at the beginning of each of his voyages of discovery. Everything he wrote began, 'In the name of the Most Holy Trinity'.

When he presented his theory of a New World waiting to be discovered he began, 'I come before you in the name of the Most Holy Trinity … to submit to your wisdom a project which has certainly come to me inspired by the same Holy Spirit.'

On the third of his great voyages, which began in 1498, he vowed to consecrate (make sacred) to the Trinity the first land that he discovered. The first island he reached was named Trinidad!

SIN

Christians believe that God sets standards for human behaviour. They call this the will of God. It is as if God sets a target for people to aim for. If they miss the target, because they are careless, or fall short of it because they don't try hard enough, this is sin. In the Gospels, the word translated as sin is the Greek word *hamartia*. It means missing the mark.

Sin is not just a list of dos and don'ts. It may have nothing to do with actions at all, but the inner thoughts and attitudes of a person. It generally means putting self first and not thinking about the feelings of others. It means to go against the will of God.

THE FALL

The Old Testament tells the story of Adam and Eve (Genesis 2–3). Many Christians view this story as symbolic. It is not a story about facts, but it tries to explain the meaning of sin.

Adam and Eve are put in a beautiful garden. There are many trees bearing fruit, including the Tree of Life, which they may eat. One fruit, however, they are not to eat. This is the fruit of the Tree of Knowledge of Good and Evil. A serpent, who represents evil, tempts them to eat the forbidden fruit. Suddenly,

The snake was the most cunning animal'

Adam and Eve are changed. They are no longer innocent and obedient. God makes them leave the Garden of Eden. The normal world is hard and tough. This is known as the **Fall**, which means the fall of humankind into disobedience and sin.

HUMAN NATURE

Christian Churches used the story of Adam and Eve to explain **original sin**. Christians in the past thought that this original sin was passed to children from their parents, in the same way as physical characteristics. Some Christians still think that all human beings are born with this badness in them.

Other Christians think the story of the Fall shows how everyone has to choose between knowledge and ignorance, good and evil. They believe that humans are born pure – like Adam and Eve in the story. Then they become influenced by the world in which they live. They are faced with anger, pride, selfishness, lust, jealousy and greed. All these negative feelings surround them, and they absorb them, sometimes without realizing it. This is how human personalities develop. From the purity of childhood people fall into selfishness and sin.

SALVATION

Christians believe that sin is failing to meet God's standards. Sin leads to estrangement (no longer being friends) between the sinner and those who are sinned against. It also breaks our relationship with God.

Salvation means wholeness, or getting right with God and with our fellow human beings.

Christians believe that only by being open to God, can they once again have a right relationship with God. They believe that God helps them to overcome sin in their lives. They may call this help **grace**, or undeserved love. This enables them to live a new and fuller life.

However, salvation does not just happen. For most people it is very hard to turn away from selfish love to the love of God and start caring about other people.

Christians believe that God's grace will only come to those who sincerely ask for it. Even so, it is not a question of working for it or training the mind.

Many Christians feel the process of salvation begins with baptism (see unit 55). This is seen as a symbolic act when the original sin that was inherited from Adam is 'washed away'.

Others feel that baptism alone is not enough. They believe that they must 'receive Jesus in their hearts'. This means they truly accept Jesus as their Lord (see unit 7). St Paul wrote to the Church at Rome:

> If you confess that Jesus is Lord and believe that God raised him from death, you will be saved. For it is by our faith that we are put right with God; it is by our **confession** that we are saved.

(Romans 10:9–10)

Many Christians believe they must give up their lives to Jesus. Then they will have everlasting life because Jesus died for their sins.

Different branches of the Church have other beliefs about salvation. **Orthodox** and Roman Catholic Christians believe that members can experience God's grace especially through the **sacraments** (see unit 41) and through the **Mass** (see unit 43). Protestants say that faith is the most important thing, and being 'right with God' comes from having faith in Jesus Christ.

KEY WORDS

Grace – the undeserved loving help that God gives to human beings
Redeemed – being reunited with God through the death of Jesus (the Redeemer) on the cross

FACTFILE

Atonement

St Paul wrote about atonement as being put right with God.

I have complete confidence in the Gospel ... For the Gospel reveals how God puts people right with himself: it is through faith from beginning to end. As the scripture says, 'The person who is put right with God through faith shall live.'... Now that we have been put right with God through faith, we have peace with God through our Lord Jesus Christ.

(Romans 1:16–17; 5:1)

POINTS OF VIEW

- Ask and you will receive: seek and you will find; knock and the door will be opened to you.

(Jesus in Matthew 7:7)

- God is ready when you are, and is waiting for you. But what am I to do, you say…? Lift up your heart to God with humble love; and mean God himself, and not what you get out of him.

(*The Cloud of Unknowing*)

INTRODUCTION

> To the Church of God which is in Corinth, to all who are called to be God's holy people … together with all people everywhere who worship our Lord Jesus Christ …
>
> (1 Corinthians 1:2)

The Church is worldwide

This was how Paul began one of his letters. From the earliest days, a Church meant a group of people, a believing community, trying to carry on the work of Jesus. The New Testament also refers to the Church as the Body of Christ. The word Church can be used in several ways:

- the worldwide Church – all Christians, everywhere

- a particular group of worshippers, for example the Roman Catholic Church, the Orthodox Church, the Methodist Church

- a building set aside for worship, which may be named after a saint or a specially holy person.

THE NICENE CREED

The Nicene Creed (see unit 21) describes the Church as one, holy, catholic and apostolic.

- One – Christians believe that God wants unity (one-ness) in the Church.

- Holy – God wants his people to be holy (which means **dedicated** to God) so that they can continue Christ's work in the world.

- Catholic – worldwide or universal, all people everywhere who worship the Lord Jesus Christ.

- Apostolic – 'from the Apostles'. Some Churches, for example Roman Catholics, **Anglicans** and Orthodox Christians, trace their history and authority back to the Apostles through their bishops. They share similar beliefs about baptism and the

Eucharist (see units 43 and 55). Other Churches feel they are also Apostolic because they follow the teachings of the Bible.

THE COMMUNION OF SAINTS

(See the Apostles' Creed, unit 5.)

The communion of saints is the close friendship shared by all Christian believers. It is also called the fellowship of believers.

The idea of the communion of saints expresses one of the mysteries of faith. Every Christian who was ever born, as well as those living and those who have not yet been born, are all members of the fellowship of believers.

In the New Testament, saints were ordinary people who had become holy. They had been sanctified (made holy) by the Holy Spirit who continues the work of Jesus. In this sense, saints are simply Christians.

In another sense, a saint may be a person who is especially holy. These saints have lived very holy lives, close to God, and are good examples for people to follow. Some of the first saints were people who died willingly for their beliefs at the time of the Roman Empire. These were called **martyrs**. Others became saints because they followed the teachings of Jesus closely in their lives.

Some Christians believe they can ask the saints in heaven to pray for them. They believe that the saints are very close to God and their prayers have special power. Some church buildings are named after particular saints. Some Christians adopt a particular saint as their patron or protector.

CANONIZATION

When a person has died, after living a very holy life, the Roman Catholic Church may consider that person is suitable to be a saint. There is a very long and complicated process before anyone can be declared a saint. **Canonization** means being officially placed on the list of saints. The **Pope** (leader of the Roman Catholic Church) makes the final decision.

In the Orthodox Church, local groups of bishops decide whether a person may be made a saint. The Anglican Church honours the saints who were canonized before the **Reformation** (see unit 21). It does not name any new saints, although many people are unofficially honoured as saints.

There is a special day in honour of all those people who have led good, saintly lives but who have not been canonized by the Church. This is the Feast of All Saints on 1 November.

Protestants generally do not agree with the idea of saints. They do not like the idea of praying to anyone except God. They fear that people might start worshipping saints and treating them as gods. Christians who do accept saints say they do not take the place of God or Jesus, and that people can still pray directly to God and Jesus.

Saint Nicholas, a Russian saint

FACTFILE

House Churches

In Britain, in the 1970–80s, a new movement started up among Christian groups. House Churches began when people started to meet in each other's homes. The movement has grown so much that many worshippers now meet in large buildings such as halls, old cinemas or rented schools. Some groups have raised enough money to build their own centres.

Worship in House Church fellowships is often more flexible, informal and personal than in some of the more traditional places of worship.

Some House Church fellowships feel they are more like the Christian Church was at the time of St Paul.

11 ETERNAL LIFE

INTRODUCTION

The Apostles' Creed (unit 5) uses the words, 'I believe in … the resurrection of the body; and the life everlasting'. The Bible says many things about the life of the world to come, or eternal life. Some of these writings are very moving.

> At once the Spirit took control of me. There in heaven was a throne with someone sitting on it … and all round the throne there was a rainbow the colour of an emerald … From the throne came flashes of lightning, rumblings and peals of thunder.
>
> (Revelation 4:2–4)

In the past, many Christians believed that heaven was somewhere above the sky. When a person died, their spirit floated up to this place to be with God. Some believed that the dead were actually raised up in new bodies. You can find both these views in the Bible. However, because the afterlife is so mysterious, they often used symbols to try to help explain it.

ST PAUL

St Paul combined these ideas in his epistles (letters).

> When the body is buried, it is mortal; when raised it will be immortal. When buried, it is ugly and weak, when raised it will be beautiful and strong. When buried, it is a physical body; when raised it will be a spiritual body.
>
> (1 Corinthians 15:42–4)

VIEWS ABOUT THE AFTERLIFE

Christians do not all agree about the afterlife. Some believe we have an immortal soul that continues to live after our bodies have died. Others think that everything we are, body and soul, dies and that what we call heaven is a new life, close to God, in a place that God has prepared for us.

JUDGEMENT

Many people often wonder at the injustice of life. What should happen to really wicked people, like Adolf Hitler? And what about the millions of innocent victims? Why do good people sometimes die young? Will there be a Day of Judgement?

In the Bible and throughout history, people have thought of hell as a place where bad people go to be punished. Good people go to heaven, while the wicked go into a lake of fire and burn for ever. The Churches used – and some Christians still use – the idea of hell to frighten people who disagreed with them. This made people feel guilty and scared. It actually put many people off Christianity.

The idea of hell as a place of eternal pain is difficult for today's Christians. They say that if God is a God of love, then how can he punish people in this cruel way? It's as if God is running an eternal torture chamber. Many Christians say that hell is a state of mind, not a place. It is being cut off from God.

Others think hell is a place where people struggle with their conscience before they can go to heaven. They are shown all the good and bad things they have done.

The afterlife?

An artist's impression of paradise

The Roman Catholic Church and some Anglicans believe in **purgatory**. This is a place where people who have not been very bad, or very good, have to go to be prepared for heaven. It is where people are purified (cleansed) from their evil. This suggests that purgatory is a temporary state, while heaven and hell are permanent.

In Matthew 25:31–46 Jesus tells the **parable** of the Last Judgement. In this parable the Son of Man (Jesus) returns to earth and judges everyone on earth. The good people stand at his right hand and go to heaven. The bad people go into the 'eternal fire which has been prepared for the Devil and all his angels'. People are judged on how they treated those in need, the sick, hungry, naked. Those who helped went to heaven. Those who closed their hearts and minds to the needs of others went into the eternal fire. Jesus said that when you help other people, you are doing it for him.

This parable stresses that salvation is open to those who follow Jesus, but also to those who do the will of God by caring for their neighbours. Many Christians believe that this shows that there is a place in the Kingdom of God for people from other faiths – and even for those who do not believe in God but who carry out his will without knowing it, by being kind to others.

THE PAROUSIA

The Apostles' Creed says that Jesus will 'come to judge the quick (the living) and the dead'. The word for the return of Christ is *parousia*, a Greek word for 'the presence'. This is part of Christian belief about the end of human history, called eschatology or 'the last things'.

For many Christians, this is an idea about the victory of good over evil, but they don't know how or when this will happen. Others believe that Christ is present, in the Spirit, now.

FACTFILE

Victory over death

The following reading from St Paul's letter to the Corinthians is often used to introduce a funeral service:

Listen to this secret truth: we shall not all die, but when the last trumpet sounds, we shall all be changed in an instant, as quickly as the blinking of an eye. For when the trumpet sounds, the dead will be raised, never to die again, and we shall be changed … then the scripture will come true: 'Death is destroyed, victory is complete! Where, Death, is your victory? Where, Death, is your power to hurt?'

(1 Corinthians 15:52–54)

Millions of Christians have very special feelings for Jesus' mother – the Virgin Mary. Thousands of churches are named after her and there are many **shrines** (small places of worship) in her honour. The Church gave Mary the title 'Mother of God' in 431 CE. Many Christians have reported seeing visions of Mary, for example, at Lourdes (see unit 54).

The Roman Catholic and Orthodox Churches give Mary special honour. They believe she can provide a link between earth and heaven. Because she is the mother of Jesus, she can intercede with him, which means she can speak on behalf of people who pray to her.

THE IMMACULATE CONCEPTION

The Roman Catholic Church teaches that Mary was born without sin and remained free from sin all her life. They believe that the Holy Spirit, rather than a man, caused Mary to conceive. Thus she remained a virgin. This is called the **Immaculate Conception**. Other Christians, think she was not necessarily a virgin, because the word in Hebrew was *Almah*, which means 'a young woman'. They stress that she was human in every way.

The Roman Catholic and Orthodox Churches teach that Mary's body was taken up into heaven when she died. They call this the Assumption of Mary. Christians celebrate this on 15 August.

MARY IN THE GOSPELS

The Gospels of Matthew and Luke record the birth of Jesus and stress that Mary was an important person. Jesus showed her respect and cared for her even as he was dying on the cross.

> Jesus saw his mother and the disciple he loved standing there; so he said to his mother, 'He is your son.' Then he said to the disciple, 'She is your mother.' From that time the disciple took her to live in his home.
>
> (John 19:26–27)

'The **Annunciation**' (when the Angel Gabriel appeared to Mary), by the painter Botticelli

Hail Mary

Hail Mary, full of grace,
the Lord is with you.
Blessed are you among women,
And blessed is the fruit of your
  womb, Jesus.
Holy Mary, Mother of God,
pray for us sinners now,
And at the hour of our death.
AMEN.

(A prayer to Mary, known as the 'Hail Mary')

FACTFILE

Feasts of Mary

Other feast days honouring Mary are her Nativity (8 September), the Annunciation (25 March), the Purification (2 February) and the Visitation (2 July).

THE VISITATION

Read this extract from the book *The Last Temptation*. How much of the story is 'real' and how much is Mary's imagination?

Mary sat on a high stool in the tiny yard of her house. She was spinning. It was still bright outside, the summer light drew slowly away from the face of the earth and did not wish to leave. Mary spun and her mind twirled now this way, now that – together with the spindle. Memory and imagination joined: her life seemed half truth, half fable.

A brilliantly white dove flew down from the roof opposite, beat its wings for a moment over her head and then alighted with dignity on the pebbles of the yard and began to walk methodically round Mary's feet. It spread its tail-feathers, bent its neck, turned its head and looked at Mary, its round eye flashing in the evening light like a ruby.

It looked at her – spoke to her. She called the bird in a very tender voice, and the delighted dove took a hop and landed on her joined knees.

Mary placed her hand on the dove which sat upon her knees. Caressing the dove, she struggled to bring the lightning back to mind after thirty years and to untangle its hidden meaning. She closed her eyes. In her palm she felt the dove's tiny warm body and beating heart … Suddenly – she did not realize how, she did not know why – dove and lightning were one; she was sure of it; the heartbeats and the thunder – all were God. Now for the first time she was able to make out the words hidden in the thunder, hidden in the dove's cooing: 'Hail Mary … Hail Mary'. Without a doubt, this was what God had cried: 'Hail Mary.'

(Nikos Kazantzakis)

INTRODUCTION

Many Christians never have any special religious experience. They never see visions, or hear voices calling to them from heaven. Their faith is quiet and simple. They believe that God came to earth and taught people how they should live their lives. Sometimes when they pray, they may feel special, as though God is close and listening to them. At worship, they may feel very happy and joyful as they sing praises to God with other Christians. Or they may believe God is present whenever human beings do work which shows great courage or self-sacrifice.

WAYS OF SEEING

Some Christians believe that the wonders of the world around them show that there is a great power at work. People can feel a sense of awe and wonder when they see nature at work, in the universe or in the birth of a baby.

'Jacob's Ladder' – Blake's idea of 'otherness'

They may have this feeling when they see the complex patterns of micro-organisms through a microscope. They may describe this feeling as a sense of 'otherness' or 'holiness'.

The English poet and artist, William Blake (1757–1827) wrote about this sense of holiness which he said we can find in the smallest things.

> To see a World in a Grain of Sand,
> And heaven in a Wild Flower,
> Hold Infinity in the palm of your hand
> And eternity in an hour.

A SENSE OF JOY AND PRESENCE

Christians may call God the 'Ultimate Reality' or the 'Holy One'. A person may experience a great joy, a powerful 'sense of presence'. A fifteen-year-old boy wrote about his experience.

> The thing happened one summer afternoon, on the school cricket field, while I was sitting on the grass, waiting my turn to bat … Suddenly and without warning, something invisible seemed to be drawn across the sky, changing the world about me into a kind of tent of concentrated and enhanced significance. What had been merely an outside became an inside. The outside world was somehow changed into something which was experienced as 'mine', but on a level where the word had no meaning: for 'I' was no longer the familiar self.

CURED BY FAITH

The New Testament has many stories about people being healed by faith.

Some people working in medicine think that if a person believes hard enough that they will get well, they might do so. More people realize that the state of the body and the state of the mind are closely related.

Some Christians are 'faith healers'. There are reports that many people have been actually healed because of their faith. We do not know what happens – whether God acts, or if faith unlocks self-healing powers within the person.

VISIONS

Visions are glimpses or pictures of especially holy or religious events or people.

The first vision described in the New Testament is when the disciples saw Jesus alive after his death. Another vision concerned Saul, who later became St Paul. At the time he had been persecuting (harassing) the early Christians.

> … suddenly a light from the sky flashed round him. He fell to the ground and heard a voice saying to him, 'Saul, Saul! Why do you persecute me?' 'Who are you, Lord?' he asked. 'I am Jesus, whom you persecute,' the voice said.'
>
> (Acts 9:3–5)

In 1858, a fourteen-year-old French girl, Bernadette Soubirous, had a very famous vision. She said that she saw the Virgin Mary several times in a cave by a river. This site is now famous as Lourdes, a place where millions of Christians go to pray to be healed. Other places have become shrines after people believed they had visions there (see unit 54).

BEING SAVED

Some people may have an experience which makes them feel an urgent need to start a new life. They feel that God, in the person of Jesus Christ, has come into their lives and they decide to 'give their lives to Jesus'. This is called conversion. They may say they have been saved or have been born again.

Converts may become very enthusiastic about their experience. Other Christians may disagree with them or become impatient with them. This may lead to arguments if 'born again' Christians claim that only people with this special experience are true Christians. These ideas can put some people off religion altogether. Many Christians think these sorts of ideas are unhelpful and wrong.

FACTFILE

Famous conversions

In 1986, the athlete Kriss Akabusi had a conversion experience at the Commonwealth Games in Edinburgh when he read the New Testament, which had been left in his hotel room. A few months later he decided to 'give his life to Jesus' and has never regretted it.

Some two hundred years before Kriss was born, John Newton, at the time the captain of a slave ship, was suddenly converted during a storm at sea. He became a clergyman, joined the fight against slavery and wrote many hymns, including 'Amazing grace, how sweet the sound.'

INTRODUCTION

Mysticism is the study of things that happen outside our ordinary, worldly existence. Mystical experiences can be strange and mysterious.

MYSTICISM IN PEOPLE'S LIVES

In all parts of the world and in all religions, people have experiences that change their lives. These experiences may be mystical. Mysticism has inspired religious teachers as well as poets, musicians, artists and architects. People describe the experience as seeing or in some way being shown things they did not understand before.

One way of describing mysticism is as a break-through where this world (the world we live in) connects with the spiritual world. The other world is one where time and ordinary things have no meaning. The other world is timeless and eternal.

THE MIDDLE AGES

In the Middle Ages, Christians thought this kind of experience was given to people to allow them to know God in a more personal way. This was called contemplation. It was a rare event, that ordinary people did not experience.

Mystical experiences may happen to anyone and may be quite unexpected. It may happen over a period of time, or only once in a life-time. When it does happen, people see things differently and may change their whole life.

> Suddenly it happened and, as everybody knows, it cannot be described in words. The Bible phrase 'I saw the heavens open' seems as good as any if not taken literally. I remember saying to myself, 'So it's like this; now I know what Heaven is like, now I know what they mean in church.' The words of the 23rd Psalm came into my head and I began repeating them: 'He maketh me to lie down in green pastures; He leadeth me beside the still waters.' Soon it faded and I was alone in the meadow with the baby and the brook and the sweet-smelling lime trees. But though it passed and only the earthly beauty remained, I was filled with great gladness. I had seen the 'far distances'.
>
> (A girl of nine – recounted in later life)

> It was during one of those recitations that, as I told you, Christ himself came down and took possession of me … [in this experience], neither my senses nor my imagination had any part; I only felt in the midst of my suffering the presence of a love, like that which one can read in the smile of a beloved face …
>
> (Simone Weil, 1909–43 – French thinker)

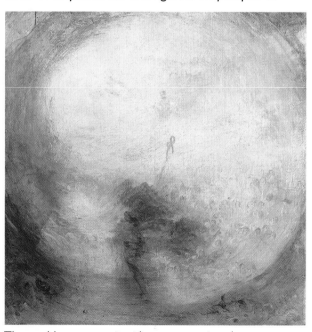

The world as we see it with our senses is only a part of reality

POINTS OF VIEW

The ideas below come from the thoughts of mystics. Some of the ideas are at the heart of Christian belief. Not all Christians agree about them.

- 'Our world' – the world we see with our senses, is only a part of reality. There is much we do not know about the universe and ourselves. We do not understand the meaning of everything.

- Humans can find out about the creator – 'God'. Intuition and feelings can help, as well as thought. Scientists often discover things by intuition and the same can happen with spiritual discovery.

- We have two 'selves'. There is the outer self, the one we carry around with us – we know and show everyone that self. But we also have another self, our true self. This true self may not be obvious – even to ourselves. It can be called spirit, soul, eternal self, the inner person, the Divine spark. We can find out about this inner self if we make the effort. We may then also 'find God'.

- If we think about it, we must realize that human life is very short and seems very unimportant compared with the vastness of the universe. What is left when we die? All our possessions and our careers will mean nothing. That is, if we only think about our 'ordinary self'. To make sense of life and to answer the question 'Why am I here?' we must seek out our 'true self'.

- All human beings have a Divine spark within them. This comes from God. Every human being can connect with the Divine. Mystics tell us our destiny is to connect with the 'other world' which is eternal and timeless.

REFLECTION

F. C. Happold, a modern writer, says that understanding and knowledge about the material world is not enough. The human spirit longs for something more. It longs for 'something which has been given many names: salvation, redemption, eternal life, the Kingdom of heaven …'

A human is a lonely being, who lives only a short time. A person is only a tiny, unimportant 'bundle of atoms in a vast, frightening, impersonal universe'. Yet this same human being is aware of a 'spark' within himself. He may think of himself as a part of the Divine Being to which he longs to return. He may share Christ's memories – then forget them and be sunk in sleep. But the divine light is there inside him, and cannot be quenched.

Suffering is part of life and no one can escape it. When others suffer, people respond in different ways. They may feel, 'It's nothing to do with me'; 'I must try to help'; 'They asked for it – it's their own fault'; 'It is through suffering that we learn to grow as human beings'.

THE PROBLEM OF EVIL

Believers and unbelievers both ask the question, 'If there is a God, why does he allow people to suffer?' Theists (people who believe in God) find this a very difficult question. If God is all-powerful he should be able to prevent evil. If he is all-loving he must be willing to prevent evil. But if God is both able and willing to prevent evil, then why does evil exist?

Christians believe that much suffering is caused by self-centredness and ignorance

Christian thinkers say that suffering has two main causes:

1 moral – caused by human sin, ignorance and selfishness

2 natural – caused by natural events such as earthquakes, disease, floods, etc.

Some Christian responses to the problem of evil are:

● After death all the suffering of this world will be forgotten in the joy of a new life.

● Suffering is caused by selfishness and self-centredness. This selfishness is sin (see unit 9). Sin is part of human nature. It does not mean doing something wrong – it is a whole attitude that keeps people away from God.

● People have free will. This means they can choose between good and evil, and between knowledge and ignorance. God does not cause suffering – human attitudes do that.

● Suffering is part of life. It challenges us and can be turned into something positive.

Although we may not understand evil, Christians believe they must do all they can to relieve suffering.

◇

POINTS OF VIEW

We must learn that to expect God to do everything while we do nothing is not faith, but superstition.

(Dr Martin Luther King)

REFLECTIONS

Human suffering, the sum total of suffering poured out at each moment over the whole earth, is like an immense ocean. But what makes up this immensity? Is it blackness, emptiness, barren wastes? No, indeed: it is potential energy.

… If all the sick people in the world were at one time to turn their sufferings into a simple shared longing for the speedy completion of the Kingdom of God … what a vast leap towards God the world would thereby make!

(Teilhard de Chardin)

Dearest Lord, may I see you today and every day in the person of the sick, and, whilst nursing them, minister unto you. Though you hide yourself behind the unattractive disguise of the irritable … the unreasonable, may I still recognize you, and say, 'Jesus, my patient, how sweet it is to serve you.'

(From the Daily Prayer, used at Mother Teresa's orphanage in Calcutta)

By suffering for us He not only provided us with an example for our imitation. He blazed a trail and if we follow it, life and death are made holy and take on a new meaning.

(Second Vatican Council – 'The Church Today')

One of my guards came to me one day and asked, 'Do you remember those first six months?' I remembered only too well! They had been horrible, cruel, and this man was the worst. 'Now,' he said, 'Abouna, dear Father, do you forgive me?' I looked at him. 'Saeed,' I said, 'I hated. I need your forgiveness.' At that moment I was free.

(Father Lawrence Jenco – hostage in Beirut)

God did not say 'You will not have a rough time; you will not be burdened; you will not have to face difficulties,' he said, 'You will not be overcome.'

(Mother Julian of Norwich – fourteenth-century English mystic)

FACTFILE

Christian aid

In 1977 a cyclone struck the coast of South India. Winds of over 240 kph tore buildings apart and a tidal wave 5.5 m high swept 4.8 km inland. By the time the cyclone ended over 25,000 people had died and more than two million were homeless. Hundreds of millions of pounds-worth of crops and buildings were destroyed.

Cyclones, typhoons and hurricanes bring suffering to millions of people every year. That is when charities such as the Red Cross, Oxfam and Christian Aid do what they can to bring relief to the suffering.

The greatest love a person can have for his friends is to give his life for them.

(John 15:13)

There have always been people who feel so strongly about something that they are prepared to give their whole lives to their beliefs. Sometimes they are willing to die for their beliefs.

When people use their lives to make the world a better place or to relieve suffering, then we should respect their sacrifice.

Martyrs are people who are willing to die for their beliefs. The gift of their life inspires others.

UNKNOWN HEROES

There are thousands of brave men and women who are not famous or well-known. Their courage and faith have inspired the lives of many others. The following prayer was found scribbled on a piece of wrapping paper near the body of a dead child at Ravensbruch, a Nazi death camp, at the end of World War II. The poet is unknown.

A prisoner's prayer

O Lord, remember not only the men
and women of good will
but also those of evil will.
But do not remember all the suffering
they have inflicted upon us;
remember the fruits we have borne
thanks to this suffering –
our comradeship, our loyalty,
our humility, our courage, our
   generosity,
the greatness of heart
which has grown out of all this;
and when they come to the judgement,
let all the fruits that we have borne
be their forgiveness.

OSCAR ROMERO

Oscar Romero was Archbishop of El Salvador. Most of the people were very poor. The country's government had no respect for human rights. It brutally crushed any opposition, so that it could keep power. Romero bravely spoke out against the government in his **sermons**. In 1980 he was shot down by four masked men while he was celebrating Mass in his cathedral. His last words were, *'May Christ's sacrifice give us the courage to offer our own bodies for justice and peace'*.

MOTHER TERESA OF CALCUTTA

This nun, who died in 1997, spent over 50 years of her life helping the very poor and the dying in Calcutta. Her Christian faith led her to live in the slums and share her life with the poor. She said,

What these people need even more than food and shelter is to be wanted. They understand that even if they only have a few hours left to live, they are loved. Make us worthy, Lord, to serve those throughout the world who live and die poor and hungry.

MAXIMILIAN KOLBE

Maximilian Kolbe was a Polish Catholic **priest**. He was taken to a Nazi death camp at Auschwitz in 1941. Thousands of people there died every day from beatings, torture, disease, starvation or in the gas chambers. Priests were especially badly treated. Once Father Kolbe was stripped naked and whipped 50 times. One day the guards took a man to be tortured to death. Father Kolbe stood up and said, 'Take me instead'. They stripped him and threw him into a stinking hole where he starved to death. He was made a saint in 1982.

1 Mother Teresa

2 Martin Luther King

3 The death of Oscar Romero

MARTIN LUTHER KING

Dr Martin Luther King was an American Baptist **minister**. He wanted to change the way that black people were treated. Despite death threats, he organized campaigns, boycotts, marches and other peaceful protests. In 1965, black people were given equal voting rights. In 1968 he was killed. He was only 39. In a speech he once said,

> I have a dream that one day all God's children, blacks, whites, Jews, Gentiles, Protestants and Catholics, will be able to join hands and sing … 'Free at last, free at last, thank God Almighty, we are free at last.'

FACTFILE

Pastor Niemoller of Wittenberg

In Nazi Germany, Pastor Niemoller of Wittenberg stood up to Hitler. He tried to encourage other pastors to stay faithful to Christ's teachings. On 1 July 1937 he was arrested and sent to a concentration camp at Dachau. He was kept isolated from other prisoners, but used the time to read and study. After the war, he became president of his Church. Nothing had separated him from God.

HUMAN PROGRESS

Today people can travel in space, transplant human organs and send messages around the world on the Internet. We have microchips and advanced computers, and can travel to anywhere in the world in a few hours. All this is part of human progress.

On the other hand, two-thirds of the world's people are hungry and wars still go on. At home, we have thousands of mentally ill people and others who simply are cruel to each other in thought, word and action. We still have a lot to learn!

PEACE OF MIND

We may ask ourselves: How can we find peace of mind in this confusing world? How can we learn to be better people? Christians believe that the teachings of Jesus Christ can help.

These teachings are found in the Gospels. Christians say they have as much meaning today as they had for the people of Jesus' day.

The teachings of Jesus have meaning for us today

JESUS CHALLENGES

Most Christians believe that Jesus was the ideal person. He represents the best example to follow. His teachings are *challenging*. This means that they are difficult to follow, and not many people have ever managed to follow them completely. These teachings are an ideal – something people should try to aim for. Read the extracts below and see how people have to change the way they think and act if they are to follow them.

> You have heard that it was said, 'Love your friends, hate your enemies.' But now I tell you: love your enemies and pray for those who persecute you.
>
> (Matthew 5:43–44)

> You must be perfect – just as your Father in heaven is perfect!
>
> (Matthew 5:48)

> Do for others what you want them to do for you.
>
> (Matthew 7:12)

> You have heard that it was said, 'An eye for an eye, and a tooth for a tooth.' But now I tell you: do not take revenge on someone who wrongs you. If anyone slaps you on the right cheek, let him slap your left cheek too.
>
> (Matthew 5:38–39)

> Do not judge others, so that God will not judge you.
>
> (Matthew 7:1)

> My commandment is this: love one another, just as I love you. The greatest love a person can have for his friends is to give his life for them. And you are my friends if you do what I command you.
>
> (John 15:12–14)

TRY HARDER

We all know of people who live out these teachings in their daily lives. Jesus teaches that people must be reborn to a new life. They must change from inside themselves. They must believe that it is possible for human beings to 'rise above' violence and unkindness and to develop as much better people.

Christians believe that if people tried harder to be like the Jesus we read about in the Gospels, then the world could begin to change for the better.

FACTFILE

The eagle of St John

Many of the quotations in this book are taken from the Gospel of St John. The symbol for this Gospel is the eagle, which flies higher than any other bird. Some people believe that the eagle is the only bird that can look straight into the sun and not be dazzled. For many Christians, the Gospel of John is the eagle of New Testament teaching. Martin Luther called it 'chiefest of the Gospels, unique, tender and true'.

TRUE HAPPINESS

Jesus begins his Sermon on the Mount in Matthew's Gospel with the **Beatitudes** (true happiness). This extract is taken from the *Good News Bible*, the version that has been used throughout this book.

Jesus saw the crowds and went up a hill, where he sat down. His disciples gathered round him, and he began to teach them:
'Happy are those who know they are spiritually poor;
the Kingdom of Heaven belongs to them!
Happy are those who mourn;
God will comfort them!
Happy are those who are humble;
they will receive what God has promised!
Happy are those whose greatest desire is to do what God requires;
God will satisfy them fully!
Happy are those who are merciful to others;
God will be merciful to them!
Happy are the pure in heart;
they will see God!
Happy are those who work for peace;
God will call them his children!
Happy are those who are persecuted because they do what God requires;
the Kingdom of Heaven belongs to them!
Happy are you when people insult you and persecute you and tell all kinds of evil lies against you because you are my followers. Be happy and glad, for a great reward is kept for you in heaven. This is how the prophets who lived before you were persecuted.'

(Matthew 5:1–12)

REFLECTIONS

Jesus taught his followers the importance of love. The highest kind of love is when you devote yourself to the wellbeing of another. This may sometimes mean giving over your whole life. Here are some readings about love.

For God loved the world so much that he gave his only son ...

(John 3:16)

Now I give you a new commandment: love one another. As I have loved you, so you must love one another.

(John 13:34)

Love is patient and kind; it is not jealous or conceited or proud; love is not ill-mannered or selfish or irritable; love does not keep a record of wrongs; love is not happy with evil, but is happy with the truth. Love never gives up; and its faith, hope and patience never fail. Love is eternal.

(St Paul: 1 Corinthians 13:4–8)

There are three words for 'love' in the Greek New Testament: one is the word 'eros'. Eros is a sort of romantic love. There is and can always be something beautiful about eros. Some of the most beautiful love in all the world has been expressed this way.

Then the Greek language talks about 'philos', which is another word for love – a kind of intimate love between friends. This is the kind of love you have for those people that you get along with well, and those whom you like on this level you love because you are loved.

Then the Greek language has another word for love, and that is the word

'**agape**'. Agape is more than romantic love, it is more than friendship. Agape is understanding, creative, redemptive goodwill towards all people. Agape is an overflowing love that seeks nothing in return. Theologians would say that it is the love of God operating in the human heart. When you rise to love on this level, you love all men not because you like them, not because their ways appeal to you, but you love them because God loves them.

This is what Jesus meant when he said, 'Love your enemies.' And I'm happy that he didn't say 'Like your enemies', because there are some people that I find it very difficult to like. ... But Jesus reminds us that love is greater than liking. Love is understanding, creative, redemptive goodwill towards all people.

(Dr Martin Luther King)

We have just enough religion to make us hate, but not enough to make us love one another.

(Jonathan Swift)

It is in the love of Jesus that you have your help. The nature of love is that it shares everything. Love Jesus and everything he has is yours.

(*The Cloud of Unknowing*)

And so I saw full surely that before ever God made us, he loved us. And this love was never quenched nor ever shall be. And in this love he has done all his works, and in this love he has made all things profitable to us, and in this love our life is everlasting.

(Mother Julian of Norwich)

When love beckons to you, follow him,
Though his ways are hard and steep.
And when his wings enfold you yield to him,
Though the sword hidden among his pinions may wound you.
And when he speaks to you believe in him,
Though his voice may shatter your dreams as the north wind lays waste your garden.
For even as love crowns you so shall he crucify you.

Even as he is for your growth so is he for your pruning.
Even as he ascends to your height and caresses your tenderest branches that quiver in the sun …
Love gives naught but itself and takes naught but from itself.
Love possesses not nor would it be possessed;
For love is sufficient unto love.

(Kahlil Gibran, 1883–1931 – Lebanese Christian, poet and artist)

FACTFILE

Mother Julian of Norwich, c.1342–1420

Mother Julian was a nun who lived alone in her cell in Norwich. In 1373, when she was 30, she received a series of sixteen visions. She then spent twenty years praying to find the meaning of these visions. Very little is known about her, but her work, *Revelations of Divine Love*, is now one of the best-loved mystical writings of all time. She was no great scholar but was certainly the first woman to write a book in the English language. Her works remained hidden for nearly 600 years, until a scholar, Grace Warrack, translated them into modern English in about 1901. Julian's main message is that 'all we are is loved by God'. She was convinced that the Creator and Redeemer of all will bring all things to perfection.

God loved the world so much that he gave his only Son

CHRISTIANITY AND SCIENCE

INTRODUCTION

Science and religion both ask questions about our universe. They also try to answer these questions.

Scientists ask 'How?' questions:

- How did this happen?
- How did this begin?
- How can we explain this?

Religions ask 'Why?' questions:

- Why did this happen?
- Why did this begin?
- Why am I here?

Hundreds of years ago, people did not distinguish between religion and science. They both dealt with the 'great unknown'. However, in the last 300 years, science has affected the way we look at life. In the twentieth century, science became very powerful. Many people think that science can explain everything. In the West, many people turn away from religion because they think that science has all the answers.

Not all scientists would agree. They realize that as new discoveries are made, old scientific laws have to be revised. Religious truths do not change in the same way. This has led to conflict between the Christian Churches and science.

CONFLICTS

We know that the universe is huge. It includes all forms of energy and matter, and things such as black holes and gravity waves. Scientists estimate that there are a hundred billion galaxies, each with a hundred million stars.

In the past, the Church taught that Earth was at the centre of the universe and everything moved around it. Galileo (1564–1642) proved that the world moved round the sun.

The Pope had him thrown into prison! The Church thought science was a threat – and this attitude lasted right up to the middle of the twentieth century.

In 1869, *On the Origin of Species* by Charles Darwin (1809–82) was published. It was about evolution and seemed to contradict the Bible's version of creation as written in Genesis 1–2. Darwin was a Christian believer. He never doubted the existence of a creator-God.

THE THREE-DECKER UNIVERSE

Many people today think that science has disproved Christianity. What it has done is to seriously question the old-fashioned picture of the universe, which was:

> God is a wise old man living up in heaven. Below the world, which 'he' created in six days burn, the everlasting fires of hell. God particularly loves the world and its peoples. The whole universe revolves around us.

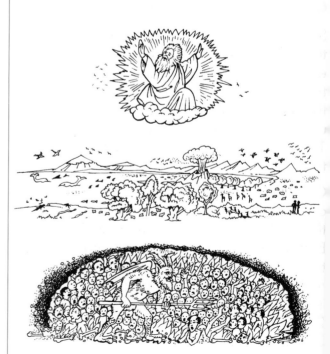

The medieval view of the universe

THE CREATION MYTH

Fundamentalist Christians (see unit 4) reject scientific theories because they believe every word of the Bible is true. Yet many Christians accept the theory of evolution as well as the Creation Story in Genesis.

The Creation Story was written down over 2400 years ago. Before that it was passed down by word of mouth for hundreds of years. Christians believe that the story is a Creation *myth*.

A myth is a way of trying to explain things which are very difficult to understand. When people cannot explain something as huge and mysterious as 'the beginning of all things', they may use picture language, or metaphors.

The Hebrew word used in the Bible for 'day' is *Yom*. When the ancient Hebrews used *Yom* they meant 'a period of time when something happens'. So six days in the Bible could just mean six periods of time during which creation took place.

ORIGINS OF THE UNIVERSE

Science has two main theories about the way the universe began. One says that it always existed. This is called the Steady State theory. However, more scientists now believe the Big Bang theory. This states that the universe began in a gigantic explosion about 18 billion years ago. These scientists also think the universe is continuing to get bigger.

Christians believe that the universe was created out of nothing. Many Christians think the Big Bang theory says the same thing. Both Christians and scientists realize they are talking about a great mystery. There are still many questions. When did time begin? What is time? Was there a Creator? Who made the Creator? Some Christians say that God (the Creator) is the One who caused everything to begin. Everything that exists only exists because of God.

RESOLUTIONS

Exciting new discoveries often bring science and religion closer together. Modern physicists have discovered atoms, nuclei, electrons, protons and neutrons and other subatomic particles. Their investigations show that the universe is a network of patterns that all link together. Everything is connected. Everything is vibrating with energy. Modern physicists are beginning to think that their discoveries are similar to the findings of the mystics in religion (see unit 14). This suggests that the universe is a living whole in which everything has meaning and purpose. Fritjof Capra, a modern physicist, writes:

> Penetrating into even deeper realms of matter, the physicist has become aware of the essential unity of all things and events … Thus the mystic and the physicist arrive at the same conclusion; one starting from the inner realm, the other from the outer world.

FACTFILE

Dom Bede Griffiths

Dom Bede Griffiths (1908–93) was a Christian monk who wrote about the apparent conflict between the material world and the world of God. 'God and the world are not two. There is no God over there, and a world over here. This is an illusion … The whole is in every part and nothing happens in any part of the universe which doesn't affect the whole … It's a marvellous vision when you think about it.'

PENTECOST

Luke wrote the book of the *Acts of the Apostles*. In it he describes a strange event that happened during the Jewish festival of **Pentecost**.

> When the day of Pentecost came, all the believers were gathered together in one place. Suddenly there was a noise from the sky which sounded like a strong wind blowing, and it filled the whole house where they were sitting. Then they saw what looked like tongues of fire which spread out and touched each person there. They were all filled with the Holy Spirit and began to talk in other languages, as the Spirit enabled them to speak.
>
> (Acts 2:1–4)

Christians do not all agree about what Luke's story means. Some believe that the events happened as described. Others believe Luke used wind and fire as symbols of the power of God. Luke goes on to describe how, by the evening of that day, over 3000 new believers had joined the Church. Luke's message is that only 50 days after the Crucifixion, Jesus' message inspired people to be his disciples. This marked the beginning of the worldwide Christian Church.

PETER AND PAUL

Jesus said to Peter, 'I tell you Peter, you are a rock, and on this rock foundation I will build my church …' (Matthew 16:18).

Peter became a very important figure in the spread of the early Church.

The other important person was Saul of Tarsus, a Jew who later changed his name to Paul. As Christianity began to spread, some people opposed it and some Christians died defending their faith. At first, Saul of Tarsus opposed the Christians and took part in the attacks on them. One day, as he was going along a road, he was blinded by a vision and heard a voice say, 'Saul, Saul, why are you persecuting me?' After this he became a follower of Jesus and spent the rest of his life travelling in the Middle East telling people about Jesus.

On his journeys he wrote many letters, called Epistles. These are in the New Testament. His letters tell the young Churches how important Jesus' message is. After many adventures, was put in prison. Eventually he arrived in Rome. He was executed in 67 CE. The Roman Emperor believed that *he* was God, not this Jewish teacher his soldiers had crucified.

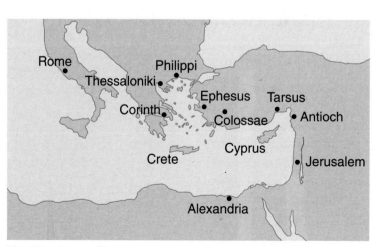

The Churches in 67 CE

WORSHIP

At first, Christians worshipped in houses or in the open air. They believed that Jesus would return soon, as the end of the world was near. There was no point in building places of worship. As time passed, leaders, called bishops, were put in charge of areas where there were groups of Christians.

Other reasons for not building churches were that the early Christians were very poor, and they were persecuted by the authorities. In the third century the Roman emperors began to tolerate the Church. In the fourth century, Emperor Constantine became a Christian and built a new city – Constantinople. Christianity became the official religion of the Roman Empire, then many churches could be built.

AUTHORITY

By 200 CE the Church was run by bishops, priests and **deacons**. These were the 'officers' of the Church. They all claimed that their authority came from Jesus, through the Apostles and Peter. This meant no one could challenge their authority to say what was true Christianity. This has continued to be an important teaching of the Roman Catholic Church to the present day.

FACTFILE

After the Apostles

Soon after the Apostles had all died, the early 'Fathers' of the Church wrote letters to the churches. *1 Clement* is a letter from the Church at Rome in about 96 CE to the Church at Corinth.

The Church at Corinth had sacked all its leaders. Clement wrote to try to sort things out. In his letter he says that God sent Christ, who sent the Apostles. They in turn selected bishops and deacons. These then chose their successors. These leaders must not be removed without just cause (good reason).

Another leader, Ignatius, wrote to the Churches about a similar problem: *'Shun divisions. Follow your bishops as Jesus Christ followed the Father. And the presbyters as the Apostles; and to the deacons pay respect as to God's commandment.'*

THE GNOSTIC GOSPELS

In 1945, an Arab peasant named Muhammad Ali found 52 papyrus texts buried in an earthenware jar at Nag Hammadi, in the Egyptian desert. These texts told about a religious movement called Gnosticism. Gnostic comes from the Greek word, *gnosis*, which means knowledge. The Gnostics claimed to have direct knowledge from Christ, by a secret route through the Apostles. Their main challenge to the Church was that they taught that Jesus did not have a human body. They said that he didn't die, but temporarily lived inside a human being.

Had they been discovered 1000 years earlier, the Gnostic texts would have been burned for their heresy ... Today we read them as a powerful alternative to what we know as orthodox Christian tradition.

(Elaine Pagels – modern theologian)

c.30: THE CHURCH IS BORN

(See unit 20).

c.70: COUNCIL IN JERUSALEM

Jesus' first disciples were Jewish. Paul wanted to include Gentiles (non-Jews). After great debate, Gentiles were allowed to join the Church.

325: COUNCIL OF NICAEA

The first Christian Emperor, Constantine, called together a worldwide (**ecumenical**) Council to decide the main teachings (doctrines) of the Church. These were mainly about Jesus: 'Is Jesus truly God?', 'Is he merely a man?' 'Is he both?' The bishops finally agreed a statement. This is now called the Nicene Creed.

381: CONSTANTINOPLE

At another Ecumenical Council the Church had to decide whether the Holy Spirit was equal to God and Jesus in the Trinity (see unit 8).

432: ST PATRICK

St Patrick (385–461) went to Ireland and set up an organized Church there.

451: CHALCEDON

There were more talks about Jesus Christ. Christians from Egypt and Syria did not agree with the main Church. Rome and Constantinople were divided. Coptic and Syrian Orthodox Churches began at this time.

540 BENEDICTINE ORDER

St Benedict, an Italian Christian, started a community of men who dedicated their lives to God. He wrote a list of rules by which all his monks had to live (see unit 35).

563 COLUMBA

Columba, a Celtic monk, started a monastery on Iona, off the west coast of Scotland. Iona became a Christian centre (see unit 28).

988: RUSSIAN ORTHODOX CHURCH

Prince Vladimir of Kiev (956–1015) was baptized and set up the Church in Russia.

1054: THE GREAT SCHISM

Ever since Chalcedon, the Pope (head of the Church in Rome) and the **Patriarch** (head of the Constantinople branch of the Church) could not agree. The Church was torn (schism means 'tear') in two. The Catholic (universal) Church was based in Rome and the Orthodox (right-thinking) Church was based in Constantinople.

1095: FIRST CRUSADE BEGINS

Christians and Muslims began a long and violent war.

1233: THE INQUISITION

The Church was sometimes very cruel and brutal. Pope Gregory IX wanted to find all **heretics** (people who did not follow the teachings of the Roman Catholic Church). He set up an

A Crusader

300 Inquisition (a court). Christian leaders justified using torture to force people to confess to being heretics. They said it was better to suffer pain on earth now than to suffer eternal torture in hell. People who were found guilty were burned at the stake.

1517: THE REFORMATION

In the Middle Ages, the Church had great power. A German priest, Martin Luther, put a notice on a church door, saying that many of the Church practices were wrong. Many people agreed. They thought the Church had forgotten the true message of Jesus. They wanted changes (reforms) so a reform movement started. This led to the start of the Protestant Churches which wanted to be free from the power of Rome.

1526: WILLIAM TYNDALE'S BIBLE

William Tyndale (1492–1536) completed his translation of the New Testament into English.

1534: KING HENRY VIII

King Henry VIII was angry with Pope Leo X because the Pope refused to let the King have a divorce. Henry made himself Head of the Church in England. This break from Rome led to the Reformation in England.

1545: THE COUNCIL OF TRENT

The Roman Catholic Church set out doctrines to protect itself against the Reformation. For the next hundred years Europe suffered wars and persecutions because of the arguments between the Churches.

1611: THE AUTHORIZED VERSION

The authorized version, also know as the King James Bible, was published.

1620: THE *MAYFLOWER* SAILS

The sailing ship *Mayflower* took Christians from Plymouth to America.

1859: CHARLES DARWIN

On the Origin of Species was published (see unit 19).

1934: THE CONFESSING CHURCH

Protestants in Germany set up the Confessing Church to stand up to Hitler's Nazis.

1948: FOUNDING OF THE WORLD COUNCIL OF CHURCHES

See unit 27.

1962–5 SECOND VATICAN COUNCIL

See unit 23.

1994: WOMEN PRIESTS

The Church of England ordained its first women priests.

KEY WORDS

Catholic	Orthodox
doctrines	Inquisition
creed	Reformation
heretic	Great Schism

FACTFILE

Constantine

It was the Emperor Constantine who called the bishops together for the Council of Nicea. He was the first emperor to take an active interest in the Church.

There are probably over 20,000 **denominations** (branches) in the Christian Church. Each denomination belongs to a larger group or family. This unit looks at the main differences. The next few units will look at the families in more detail.

The Families of Christianity
It helps to know how each of the three main traditions or groups began.

500

In early days, the Church had an Eastern (Greek-speaking) tradition and Western groups based in Rome.

Byzantine (Greek) Church survived Islamic threat.
Orthodox churches in Greece, Russia, etc.

1054 The Great Schism: East and West separate

1517 Luther's 95 Theses: the Reformation begins

1000

Strong Church: many abuses.

1500

Counter-Reformation.

Many protestant groups: Anglicans, Lutherans, Reformed. Later Baptists, Methodists, Quakers, etc.

CATHOLICISM   PROTESTANTISM   ORTHODOXY

	The Roman Catholic Church	The Protestant (Reformed) Churches and groups	The Orthodox Churches
What are they?	All Christians who accept the authority of the Pope (Bishop of Rome, see unit 23).	All Christian groups who came after the Reformation. Includes Anglicans, Baptists, United Reformed, Methodists, Quakers, Lutherans, Pentecostal, Salvation Army (see unit 25).	Sometimes called 'eastern' Orthodox. At first led by the Patriarch of Constantinople. Now fifteen Orthodox Churches include Russian, Greek and Churches.
How are they organized?	The Pope is the head and under him are cardinals, archbishops, bishops and priests. Also has 'orders' of monks and nuns.	Each denomination has its own local, national or international organization. Most belong to the World Council of Churches. (see unit 27).	Each Church is self-governing and run by its own Patriarch. Under him are bishops and priests. They also have monks and nuns.
What things do they emphasize?	The authority of the Pope. To be the one true Church. The seven sacraments (see unit 41). The Mass is the most important one.	The importance of the Bible, not the traditions of any Church. The authority of the Bible does not need the Church to interpret it.	They have the 'true' faith, beliefs and practices, handed down by Jesus himself to his Apostles (see unit 24).

The divisions within Christianity have led to a lot of violence and tragedy. Time and again the Church has gone against the teachings of Christ. People have died rather than change from one denomination to another. To this day, there are often violent divisions in Croatia between Orthodox Christians and Catholics. Northern Ireland has shown how some Protestant and Roman Catholics have abused the Christian religion.

THE ECUMENICAL MOVEMENT

In the twentieth century the Church tried to spread the Gospel through the work of missionaries. They found this difficult to do from a divided Church, so a movement began to bring unity. This is called the Ecumenical Movement. Its aim is to encourage the various families of Churches to co-operate in worship and service, and to try to understand each other.

THE WORLD COUNCIL OF CHURCHES

The World Council of Churches (WCC, see unit 27) has had great influence on the Ecumenical Movement. The WCC was founded in Amsterdam in 1948. It has representatives from Orthodox and Protestant Churches, and acts as a united force for Christianity in the world. It is concerned with both religious and social issues. For example, it looks at racism, the arms trade, human rights and world poverty. Some people think the WCC spends too much time on political issues, but many Christians see working for peace and justice as part of their faith. The WCC claims to represent over 400 million Christians. It sees itself as a fellowship of Churches. The Roman Catholic Church is not a member of the WCC.

THE PAN-ORTHODOX CONFERENCE

This was set up in 1961 by the Orthodox Churches for friendly discussions with non-Orthodox Christians. It aims to promote unity.

QUOTES

- A cynic might say that the Churches are coming together to fight for survival, at a time when their influence and numbers are declining. But it is also the case that many exciting and creative things are happening at all levels of the Church.

  (Dr Lorna Brockett)

- For the first time in history … [the Ecumenical Movement] … has now taken on the character of an urgent desire for world peace. It can help to make our earth more liveable, by making it more peaceful and reconciled.

  (Hans Küng, *Christianity and the World Religions*, 1987)

FACTFILE

What is Ecumenical?

'Ecumenical' comes from the Greek word *oikoumene*. This meant 'the inhabited world'. Activities that mean Christians unite, to work together, are called ecumenical. The idea is that people come together from a wide area and from different Churches.

Roman Catholics believe that the Pope (the Bishop of Rome) can trace a direct link back to Peter, the disciple. The Pope has special authority to decide on Christian matters, and the local bishops share this authority. The Roman Catholic Church believes that this authority ensures that Jesus' teachings are protected and are understood correctly. Many Roman Catholics believe that when the Pope speaks to the Church, or in its name, he is **infallible** (never wrong).

Roman Catholics learn about their Church and doctrines through the **catechism**. This is a question-and-answer teaching system. These are some of the beliefs.

> Christ Jesus gave himself for us to redeem us from all iniquity (sin) and to purify for himself a people of his own.
>
> (Titus 2:14)

> You are a chosen race, a royal priesthood, a holy nation, God's own people.
>
> (1 Peter 2:9)

> The Church is the Body of Christ. Through the Spirit and his action in the sacraments, above all the Eucharist, Christ, who once was dead and is now risen, establishes the community of believers as his own Body.

> In the unity of this Body, there is a diversity of members and functions. All members are linked to one another, especially to those who are suffering, to the poor and persecuted …

> The Church is the Bride of Christ: he loved her and handed himself over for her. He has purified her by his blood and made her the fruitful mother of all God's children.

> … the universal Church is seen to be 'a people brought into unity from the unity of the Father, the Son and the Holy Spirit.'
>
> (Catechism of the Catholic Church, 1994)

THE SECOND VATICAN COUNCIL

In 1962, Pope John XXIII, called together 2600 Roman Catholic churchmen to meet at the Vatican. There were bishops, cardinals, abbots and heads of religious orders. This was the Second Vatican Council. (The First Vatican Council was in 1869.)

The aim of the Second Vatican Council was to bring the Church up to date and to get in touch with people and the problems they face in modern times. Pope John had already set up a study group to look at relations between the Roman Catholic Church and other Churches – the Secretariat for promoting Christian Unity.

John XXIII died in 1963, but the next Pope, Paul VI, continued the work of the Council.

WHAT DID THE SECOND VATICAN COUNCIL ACHIEVE?

- For the first time the Roman Catholic Church listened to other Christian Churches. They condemned past intolerance and persecutions.

- Before the Council, worship was in Latin. Since then, worship has been in languages people understand.

- There was less Church censorship of books and teachers had more freedom.

- The Council looked at political and social issues. They discussed nuclear weapons,

Pope John XXIII

the arms trade, poverty, racism and the communist world.

They planned greater tolerance to other world religions.

These were all new – but many of the Church's teachings remained the same.

They kept the idea that the Pope was infallible.

Beliefs about the Virgin Mary (see unit 12) didn't change.

Artificial forms of contraception were condemned (see unit 57).

Abortion was seen as 'an evil that poisons society' (see unit 70).

THE COUNCIL SAID ...

- We must not remain indifferent to those communities whose citizens suffer from poverty, misery and hunger.

- The arms race should cease ... nuclear weapons should be banned.

- Virginity must be regarded as a gift from God.

- From the moment of conception life must be guarded with the greatest care.

FACTFILE

Hans Küng – Catholic writer

Hans Küng was born in 1928 in Lucerne in Switzerland. He studied to become a priest and wrote many influential books. In his most popular book *On Being a Christian* he tried to answer the questions, 'Why be a Christian? Why not simply aim at being genuinely human?' He decided that it was only by being truly Christian that we can be fully human. He made himself unpopular with Church leaders when he questioned the idea that the Pope was infallible. He wrote, 'The Pope exists for the Church, and not the Church for the Pope. His primacy is ... the primacy of service. He ... must not set himself up as overlord either of the Church or of the Gospel ...'

IN BRIEF

The headquarters of the Roman Catholic Church is in Rome, Italy. The Pope lives in the Vatican – a walled 'city-within-a-city' in Rome. Its main cathedral is St Peter's.

At one time all Christians were part of one Church. After the Great Schism in 1054 (see units 21 and 22) the Orthodox and Catholic Churches broke away from each other.

There are Orthodox Christians in every part of the world. In some countries the national Church is Orthodox. The Byzantine (Greek and Russian) Orthodox are well-known to most people in the West, but there are also the Oriental (eastern) Orthodox Churches of Syria, Ethiopia, Armenia, South India, and the Coptic Church in Egypt. There are many Orthodox communities in Britain and other parts of the world.

ORTHODOX BELIEFS AND CUSTOMS

Most Christians share beliefs about the teachings of Jesus and the nature of God. The Orthodox Churches have few differences. They believe in the Trinity: God the Father, creator of all things; God the Son, who became man, died for our sins and rose again from the dead; and God the Holy Ghost, the Spirit of Truth who fills all things. They believe that Jesus was truly God and truly human. He was born to the Virgin Mary, whom they call *Theotokos* (Mother of God). These beliefs are set out in the Creed.

They believe that it is not enough to go to Church regularly, important though this is. If people claim to believe in Jesus Christ they must change their life and behaviour and try to become holy, as Jesus is holy. This spiritual struggle is hard. People cannot make it on their own. They need to work with God. By allowing God to work in them, people can be **transfigured** (transformed, made holy) by allowing God's love to shine through them.

Orthodox Christians believe that Jesus was the true image of God, and that we are meant to be like him. In humans, God's image has been distorted. It has been twisted

An Orthodox church in Russia

through sin. We must try even harder to restore the image of God in ourselves by rejecting sin.

Believers must answer difficult moral questions according to what their own conscience tells them, through prayer. However, they will need guidance from the Church because it is human nature to make mistakes.

ORTHODOX WORSHIP AND THE SACRAMENTS

Orthodox churches are often very beautifully decorated and have many **icons**, or pictures of holy men and women. These help believers to focus on their worship. Orthodox choirs are also known for their very beautiful singing 'like the choirs of Heaven'.

Orthodox Christians believe that Jesus left the Holy Sacraments to help his followers become more aware that God is among them. The most important is the Holy Eucharist, when believers share the Body and Blood (see units 41 and 43). This is part of the Divine **Liturgy** (holy service).

When new members join the Church, they receive the sacraments of baptism (washing away sins) and **chrismation** (receiving the Holy Spirit by being anointed with holy oil).

Other Sacraments are **ordination** (when men are made bishops, priests or deacons by the laying on of hands), marriage (the blessing of the union between man and woman); Confession (being forgiven one's sins) and holy unction (anointing a sick person with holy oil).

Orthodox worshippers believe that God is specially 'present' on each of these occasions and gives his grace and blessing to believers.

For Orthodox Christians, the sense of mystery is a very important part of their belief and worship (see unit 14).

> God cannot be understood through human reason, which is limited, or through the senses, which are liable to error, but … through our spiritual understanding, which can glimpse beyond what appears on the surface. Through prayer and stillness we can gradually come closer to God … Many Orthodox Christians use the beautiful 'Jesus Prayer' ('Oh Lord Jesus Christ, Son of God, have mercy on me, a sinner') as a means of focusing their whole being on God. This wonderful prayer originated in monasteries.
>
> (Father Gregory Wirdnam, British Orthodox priest)

QUOTES

- We know that our life is temporary, and we had better live with Christ and offer ourselves, and have true life in him.

  (Pope Shenouda III – leader of the Egyptian Coptic Church)

- The object of our search is the fire of grace which enters into the heart … When the spark of God Himself – grace – appears in the heart, it is the prayer of Jesus which fans it into flame … The essential thing is to hold oneself ready before God, calling out to Him from the depths of one's heart.

  (Bishop Theophanes)

- An icon or a cross does not exist simply to direct out imagination during prayers. It is a material centre in which there rests … a divine force, which unites itself to human art.

  (Vladimir Lossky)

FACTFILE

'It's all Greek to me!'

'Orthodox' comes from the Greek words *orthos* meaning right and *doxa* meaning belief. The Eastern Orthodox Church is a group of Churches, each with its own Patriarch. The name 'patriarch' comes from another Greek word meaning father. The ancient Greek Church is sometimes called the Byzantine Church. Byzantium is the old (Greek) name for Constantinople – which is now called Istanbul!

In this unit we look at some of the main features of the largest Protestant Churches.

THE LUTHERAN CHURCH

There are about 70 million Lutherans today. They are mainly in German-speaking countries, and in Scandinavia and North America. They follow the teachings of Martin Luther (1483–1546). They believe in *justification by faith*. This means that God gives his grace (blessing) to those who have faith. They do not have to deserve it. They also believe that the Bible contains all that they need to know to achieve this faith.

In their worship, they value good preaching, the sacraments, Bible-reading and **hymn**-singing. They have male and female priests.

THE REFORMED CHURCHES

This family of Churches follows the teachings of one of the early reformers, John Calvin (1509–64). The Reformed Churches include the Presbyterian Churches, Congregational Churches and some Baptist groups.

There are Reformed Churches in Britain, throughout Europe and North America, and in most other parts of the world.

Their teachings stress the Bible, the rule of God, justification by faith and Jesus as head of the Church. There are three types of leader in Reformed Churches: ministers or presbyters, elders and deacons.

THE FREE CHURCHES

During the seventeenth and eighteenth centuries many Churches broke away from the English-speaking Churches. They are known as the Free Churches. The best known include the Baptists, the Methodists, the Pentecostal Churches, the Salvation Army and the Religious Society of Friends (also known as Quakers).

The Baptists

There are about 32 million Baptists. They earned their name because they practise believers' baptism. Only people who are old enough to understand and accept the Christian faith and 'give themselves to Jesus' are baptized (see unit 55). They also believe in the priesthood of believers. This means that all members take part in every aspect of the life of the Church.

The Methodists

John and Charles Wesley, founded the Methodist Church in the eighteenth century. They thought that Anglican worship was too formal and they wanted to have a simpler form of service. The first words in the Methodist hymn book are, 'Methodism was born in song'. This says a great deal about the Methodist Church. The Wesleys wrote some of the best hymns in the Christian religion. They wanted to 'inject some life into services'. Services are made up of hymn-singing, prayers, Bible readings and a sermon.

The Pentecostal Churches

The Pentecostal Church takes its name from the day of Pentecost, when the first Christians received power from the Holy Spirit (see unit 20). Pentecostalists believe in the 'baptism of the Holy Spirit', a personal experience of God. Many believe that speaking in tongues (*glossolalia*) is evidence of a close relationship with God. They are keen **evangelists** (spreading the message) and send missionaries around the world.

The Salvation Army

William Booth (1829–1912) was a Methodist minister who worked in the slums of Victorian England. He said, 'Why should the devil have all the best tunes?' Music is very important to the Army's worship and every service or open-air meeting is filled with the sound of brass bands, hand-clapping and singing of songs (hymns).

Salvation Army bands are a common sight

The Army is built on military lines. The men and women who act as ministers are 'officers', members are 'soldiers' and they all wear uniforms. Their meeting-place is called a Citadel. The Salvation Army works all over the world among the poor and under-privileged.

The Society of Friends (Quakers)

George Fox (1624–91) was the founder of the Society of Friends. He was given the nickname of Quaker after he told a judge to quake and fear at the word [of God]'. Quaker worship is very simple. They have no creed, sacraments, priests, ordered services or special buildings. In their service, silence is important (see unit 42). Quakers believe that God speaks directly to the hearts of believers.

The Evangelicals

This is one of the fastest-growing groups in Christianity today. They believe that faith, studying the Bible and learning about the religion are more important than ceremonies. They aim to convert those who hear them preach about the 'good news'. They insist that the Bible is the inspired word of God and that people need a personal relationship with Jesus Christ through being 'born again'.

FACTFILE

George Fox , 1624–91

If you visit Launceston in Cornwall, you will find the remains of a prison cell in which George Fox, founder of the Quakers, was imprisoned for a time. Altogether he spent six years in different prisons for preaching that truth is to be found in God speaking to the human soul. Prison conditions in those days were terrible. George Fox campaigned against this and against other social evils. He set up schools in his later years and he worked both in the north of England and in London.

The enthronement of the Archbishop of Canterbury

The Anglican Church began when the Church in England separated from the Church of Rome in the sixteenth century (see unit 21). The Church in England rejected the Pope. The monarch became the head of the Church. This link between Church and State is called 'establishment'. It still exists in England, though not in Wales. Bishops of the established Church have seats in the House of Lords and can take part in government.

Anglican Churches differ in their approach to Christian teachings. Some are Protestant in their teachings and practices. Others are much closer to the Roman Catholic tradition. These may even call themselves Anglo-Catholics. All Anglicans agree that their Church is part of the 'holy Catholic Church' described in the Creeds, but it is not part of the Roman Catholic Church.

> At its best … the Anglican Church … tries to hold together the more Catholic traditions; the evangelical emphasis on the Bible and personal conversion and openness to new ideas.
>
> (Donald Coggan, former Archbishop of Canterbury)

Despite wide differences in practice, the Anglican Churches agree that:

- the Holy Scriptures contain everything necessary for salvation
- the Apostles' Creed and the Nicene Creed express the Christian faith
- the two sacraments of Baptism and the Lord's Supper (Communion) are recognized
- their bishops are in direct line from the Apostles (the Apostolic succession).

A WORLDWIDE CHURCH

Anglican Churches exist mainly in countries which were once British but are now independent, such as the USA, Australia and Canada. Now the largest Anglican population overseas is in Africa. Altogether there are over 750 Anglican **dioceses** throughout the world. A diocese is a group of churches headed by a bishop. The spread of the Anglican Church is due largely to the work of the Church Missionary Society.

The Anglican Communion (family) respect the Archbishop of Canterbury as their leader, not as their ruler. The Churches meet every ten years at the Lambeth Conference (Lambeth Palace is the Archbishop's London home). This conference also celebrates the unity of the Churches.

THE CHURCH AT WORK

The Anglican Church cares about the society in which we live. It has many organizations concerned with helping people who are in trouble.

- The Children's Society (see unit 64) runs adoption agencies, schools and nurseries for disabled children, gypsy playgroups, hostels for single parents and their babies, as well as welfare schemes for deprived children.

The Church Army has about 150 officers. They help the aged, run housing schemes and hostels for the homeless and work with prisoners.

ANGLICAN WORSHIP

All Anglicans believe that worship is at the heart of their life and **mission**. Until about 1980 all Anglicans used a version of *The Book of Common Prayer*, first used in the sixteenth century. Now there is more variety in Anglican services, but some elements of the old prayer book are still very important in Anglican worship.

Another recent change in Anglican worship is the ordination of women in most provinces (districts) of the Anglican Communion. The first women priests were ordained in England in 1994.

Anglicans think that the Eucharist, or Holy Communion is very important (see unit 43). Many Anglicans also attend the offices (services) of matins (morning prayer) and evensong.

Anglicans have developed a distinctive style of worship. They sing Psalms (found in the Bible) and canticles (short religious songs based on verses from the Bible). Some of the chants (tunes or settings) are very old, and possibly date from the earliest days of the Church. Others are modern and have been composed especially for church choirs.

One well-known canticle is the *Magnificat*. It is taken from Luke's Gospel.

MAGNIFICAT

My soul doth magnify the Lord, and my
    spirit hath rejoiced in God my Saviour.
For he hath regarded the lowliness of his
    hand-maiden.
For behold from henceforth all
    generations shall call me blessed.

For he that is mighty hath magnified me,
    and holy is his name.
And his mercy is on them that fear him
    throughout all generations.
He hath showed strength with his arm:
    he hath scattered the proud in the
    imagination of their hearts.
He hath put down the mighty from their
    seat and hath exalted the humble and
    meek.
He hath filled the hungry with good
    things and the rich he hath sent empty
    away.
He remembering his mercy hath helped
    his servant Israel;
As he promised to our forefathers,
    Abraham and his seed, for ever.
Glory be to the Father, and to the Son
    and to the Holy Spirit;
As it was in the beginning, is now and
    ever shall be: world without end.
    Amen.

(Luke 1:46–55)

FACTFILE

Anglican prayers

Anglicans use a Prayer Book to help them in their worship. This prayer asks for God's help to be better Christians.

Teach us, good Lord, to serve thee as thou deservest; to give, and not to count the loss; to fight and not to heed the wounds; to toil, and not to seek for rest; to labour, and not to ask for any reward save that of knowing that we do thy will; through Jesus Christ our Lord. Amen.

(Alternative Service Book)

The World Council of Churches (WCC) was formed in 1948 as:

> ... a fellowship of Churches which confess the Lord Jesus Christ as God and Saviour according to the scriptures and therefore seek to fulfil together their common calling to the glory of the One God, Father, Son and Holy Spirit.

Apart from the Roman Catholic and some Evangelical Churches, all the main Christian Churches belong to the WCC. The Roman Catholic Church sends official observers to the general assemblies (meetings) of the WCC. The assemblies are attended by thousands of delegates from hundreds of Churches throughout the world. They discuss many different issues.

One topic of discussion has been Church unity. Few Church mergers have actually taken place, but Churches are now far more prepared to listen to one another.

Another topic has been 'the needs of a torn world' and for this reason the WCC has sometimes been accused of being too political.

The WCC's main areas of work are:

- faith and order – making people aware of the Christian message and working for unity among the Churches
- life and work – helping to bring peace and social justice in the world.

FACTFILE

Words and deeds

When the WCC met in 1975, its theme was 'Jesus Christ Frees and Unites'. It was concerned with 'the whole Church bringing the whole Gospel to the whole person in the whole world.' But words alone were not enough, they said.

Christians are called ... to proclaim the Gospel to the ends of the earth. Simultaneously, we are commanded to struggle to realize God's will for peace, justice and freedom ...

(*Confessing Christ Today*)

'There is a great divide between North and South, between East and West.'

REFLECTIONS

One World, the WCC Magazine, reported on an Assembly with the theme 'Jesus Christ, the Life of the World'. The Assembly wanted to talk about Christians living together and working together to make things better for Christ's world.

'We hear the cries of millions who face a daily struggle for survival … We see the camps of refugees and the tears of all who suffer inhuman loss. We sense the fear of rich groups and nations and the hopelessness of many … who live in great emptiness of spirit. There is a great divide between North and South, between East and West. Our world – God's world – has to choose between "life and death, blessing and curse" …'

The report says that the misery and chaos of the world come from people turning away from God. People no longer work together. People can learn how God meant us to live by looking at the life of Jesus. 'He experienced our life, our birth and childhood, our tiredness, our laughter and tears. He shared food with the hungry, love with the rejected, healing with the sick, forgiveness with the penitent …'

It says that divisions within the Church show how Christians fail to obey God. They cling to old prejudices. Yet God still gives his grace (blessing) to the Church. 'One sign of this grace is the Ecumenical Movement in which no member of the Church stands alone.

'The Assembly therefore renews its commitment to Church unity. We take slow, stumbling steps on the way to the visible unity of the Church …'

The report goes on to say that this hope of unity enables the Church to continue its work of telling the world about '… the Good News that Jesus Christ, God and Saviour, is the Life of the World … we must remember that God's love is for everyone, without exception …'

The Assembly also renewed its commitment to justice and peace. They believe that Jesus Christ served the whole of life, and so the Church must serve the life of all. God's gift of life is attacked by the powers of death. 'Injustice denies God's gifts of unity, sharing and responsibility. When nations, groups and systems hold the power of deciding other people's lives, they love that power. God's way is to share power, to give it to every person …

'The arms race everywhere consumes great resources that are desperately needed to support human life. Those who threaten with military might are dealing in the politics of death. It is a time of crisis for us all. We … call persistently, in every forum, for a halt to the arms race. The life which is God's gift must be guarded when national security becomes the excuse for arrogant militarism … Life is given. We receive God's gift with constant thankfulness.'

The writer expresses surprise that God trusts ordinary people the way he does. 'That is the risk God takes. The forces of death are strong. The gift of life in Christ is stronger. We commit ourselves to live that life, with all its risks and joys, and therefore dare to cry, with all the host of heaven "O death, where is your victory?" Christ is risen. He is risen indeed.'

In this unit we look at two Christian communities that show how ecumenism (Christian unity) works in the world today.

IONA

Iona is an island off the west coast of Scotland. In 563 CE St Columba arrived there to begin his mission to Scotland and the north of England.

George Macleod, a Scottish minister, founded the Iona Community in 1938. Macleod wanted to form a community where people from all walks of life could come together to live, work and worship. With his fellow-workers, Macleod rebuilt the abbey on the island and the community grew. Members pray for half an hour each morning. They study the Bible and give five per cent of their money to the community. They try to live together by following Christian ideals. There are also thousands of Associate Members who attend the youth camp. The Reflection on this page is an account of a visit by a sixteen-year-old girl.

The abbey of St Columba, Iona

REFLECTION

Iona struck me almost immediately as being a beautiful and special place. The light is so bright, the sea so wild and the weather so changeable. We were met from our small boat by two community members who took us to the restored abbey. After dinner we introduced ourselves – everyone was so friendly and we were given our little chores for the week.

During the week we had talks and discussions about all sorts of things, especially about world poverty and world peace. We learnt about how the work of Iona goes on in the slums of Glasgow and we felt the commitment of the people living on Iona. After a week there I felt rested both in body and mind. In a strange sort of way I felt that I had experienced a force greater than myself – I call this force God.

(Visitor to Iona)

TAIZÉ

That Christ may grow in me, I must know my own weakness and that of my brothers. For then I will become all things to all, and even give my life, for Christ's sake and the Gospel's.

(From *The Rule of the Community*)

Taizé is a community of Christian monks in a small village in France. The community was founded in 1940 by Roger Schutz. He believed there was a need for a new kind of monastic life within the Protestant Church (see unit 35). The members of the Taizé community take vows of poverty, chastity and obedience.

he brothers take care of thousands of sitors every year. They also run their own rinting press, a farm and a pottery. Every ear, thousands of young people from all ver the world camp in the fields around the monastery. They take part in worship and discussions and they do manual work.

The Reflection below is an account of one person's visit to Taizé.

REFLECTION

The Church of Reconciliation ... was dark, cool and crowded. We sat on the carpeted floor. It was quiet; the brothers in robes knelt or sat in a wide line down the centre of the church. The service began. We sang, listened to Bible readings in several languages, and prayed ... then a long period of silence and meditation followed. To sit on the floor ... in silence – this was very powerful. I could feel the silence. After this, you could take communion, Roman Catholics on one side of the church, the rest on the other ...

Lying on my bed, I found that events of the day flashed by, as did the week ...

What remains in my mind? – the weekly Easter perhaps! ... the church is jam-packed on Fridays as the cross is laid flat on the floor, prayers are offered for persecuted Christians and for those who are prisoners of conscience. You may press your head to the cross as a sign to commit all that weighs you down to Christ.

It is sad to leave ... It wasn't the personality of Brother Roger, nor the brothers, nor the place, nor even all the people I had shared my life with for a week. In some way it was all of them rolled into one. To be part of something living, vital ... makes you vital too.

(Visitor to Taizé)

FACTFILE

More about Taizé

The founding of Taizé was no easy task. Roger Schutz, its present Prior, began by taking Jewish and other refugees into his home at Taizé in Burgundy in 1940. In 1942 the Gestapo found out and forced him to leave, but in 1944 he returned with three Brothers to begin his new community. By 1949 the first monks arrived and took vows of poverty, chastity and obedience.

Now there are more than 70 men from different traditions, including Franciscan and Orthodox monks. Since 1968, Roman Catholics have also joined. Taizé is now truly ecumenical. It has links with the Roman Catholic, Orthodox, Anglican and Free Churches. Brothers also attend the World Council of Churches.

INTRODUCTION

For many years Northern Ireland has been torn apart by political divisions. People say that the root cause of the trouble is the religious differences between Roman Catholics and Protestants.

WORKING FOR PEACE

One religious community – Corrymeela – is trying to work for peace. Corrymeela was founded in 1965 by a chaplain called Ray Davey and by Christians – Catholics and Protestants – who wanted to heal the divisions. The main site is at Ballycastle on the Antrim coast.

There are 140 members and over 1000 'friends' who work for reconciliation (bringing people back together), to re-establish friendship between groups. In any year 8000 people from a variety of backgrounds visit Corrymeela. Each group stays for between two days and a week. The groups may be families under stress, bereaved families, families of prisoners, single-parent groups, school, youth or church groups – the list is endless.

THE SEED GROUPS

An important part of the work at Corrymeela is aimed at helping young people to understand themselves, their relationships and their communities. The Corrymeela community runs seed groups. These are groups of up to twenty people, between the ages of 18 and 21, meeting every weekend for six months.

Reverend Douglas Baker, a Corrymeela worker, explains the idea of the seed groups.

> Jesus uses the way seeds grow as a parable to help his followers understand how God's kingdom grows in the world. It is a powerful message of hope ... The aims we have identified for the seed groups are:
>
> - **reflecting** on all the events which have shaped who we are, on the issues and choices which confront us in terms of who we shall become
>
> - **understanding** ourselves and our relationships with others
>
> - **relating** the Christian faith to our own experience
>
> - **building bridges** of trust, understanding and personal friendship
>
> - **encouraging** the development of ideas for reconciliation.

Many Christians pray that the deep divisions within Northern Ireland may at last be healing

KEY IDEAS

Corrymeela is a symbol that Catholics and Protestants can work together in real Christian fellowship.

It is a channel through which all sorts of people can work together ...

It is a challenge not to surrender to apathy or despair but to work courageously for peace and understanding wherever we are.

(Corrymeela leaflet)

REFLECTION 1

Aine went to Corrymeela after her son was murdered.

I was just having a wee cry in the kitchen. Mostly now I'm all right but sometimes it comes over me round this time – when he'd be comin' in for his supper with his dad … And you know how a lad likes his food – he'd say 'Great, Mum! It's onions tonight and you've been cryin'!' … It was Corrymeela got me where I am now. I never felt at Mass what I felt at those prayers together in Corrymeela. Protestants and Catholics we were, all together, and the Protestants knew 'twas theirs killed my son and they prayed special for me – and it worked! I'll never be happy again, see. But I'm not angry no more.

REFLECTION 2

Dorothy Wilson, a Corrymeela member, is involved in integrated (mixed) schools for Protestant and Catholic children.

She believes it is vital for Protestant and Catholic children to be educated together. With the long-standing conflict in Northern Ireland, the two sides often know very little about each other. She feels that children could attend these new schools without losing any of their religious identity. Then, if children went to school together, some of their ignorance about each other might be overcome.

REFLECTION 3

Barry is a Catholic and a Nationalist.

At Corrymeela I met [Protestants] who live in the same town as me and whom I had never talked with before. The discussions were initially very wary. Deep emotions were stirred in me, but soon … we were sharing our different views and experiences. I was overwhelmed at what came out and how people listened to one another. At the end of the weekend I went along with the others to the short Corrymeela Community service. At the finish we were invited to say the Our Father (the Lord's Prayer). We took hands and during the prayer I began to cry … I have never experienced anything like it before. It was also the first time in my life I had ever prayed with Protestants.

FACTFILE

Women of peace

In 1977 the Nobel Peace Prize was awarded to Betty Williams and Mairead Corrigan. In August 1976 a terrorist getaway car hit and killed three children. The children's aunt, Mairead, and her friend Betty decided they would do something. Despite threats from terrorists they demanded peace. They formed the Ulster Peace Movement. On Good Friday, 1998, a peace agreement was signed. This brought hope that the Seeds of Peace of Corrymeela and the Ulster Peace Movement had begun to grow.

White missionaries with their converts

Jesus said, 'Go then, to all peoples everywhere and make them my disciples.'

(Matthew 28:19)

Christians believe that God sent his son, Jesus Christ, so that people could be saved. Many think they should share their beliefs with everyone, all over the world. Missionaries are people who go to non-Christian groups to try to convert them to Christianity. Christian missionaries work in many places in the world. They try to help people to come to know Jesus Christ and accept him into their hearts.

There are three different ideas about mission and the task of the Church.

1 The task of the Church is to convert people and make them members of the Church so that they can be 'saved'.

2 The Church should set up Christian communities in new places. Local people should decide for themselves and run their own Churches.

3 It is not up to the Church to convert people.

'WHITE SOULS'

During the seventeenth to nineteenth centuries, Europe was very rich and powerful It began to see the world as a place where they could make a lot of money. They colonized (took over) much of America, Africa and the East. The set up businesses and these were protected by European rmies. Then the Christian missionaries ame. They often seemed to think that illions of 'unfortunate natives' needed to be onverted from their own religions. The issionaries also taught European values nd morals, as if these were the same as odliness.

Many missionaries seemed to want to plant white souls' inside dark-skinned bodies. Missionaries were seen as symbols of white upremacy. They exploited (took advantage f) native peoples. Early missionaries often gnored the richness of the native peoples' wn history, culture and religions.

ome people applied Darwin's theory of the urvival of the fittest to humans. Western aces had advanced technology and greater wealth and power, so they must be the fittest. This arrogance and ignorance caused a great deal of suffering for peoples in the olonies.

On the other hand, many missionaries worked to stop slavery. They brought benefits o the people, such as medical services and public education. By the 1920s, many missionaries were beginning to see that their most important task was to help the peoples of Africa to prepare for self-government.

A MULTI-FAITH SOCIETY

n modern Britain, many people follow eligions other than Christianity. This has esulted in a change of attitude about missionary work. There are two opposing views.

1 All religions can lead to salvation. The Church's task is to understand others, to learn from them and share ideas. Its job is not to convert others, but to show by example how true Christians live and so bear witness to Jesus Christ.

2 The only way to God is through belief in Jesus Christ. Followers of other religions are not wrong, but can only go part-way to understanding God.

POINTS OF VIEW

Wherever you find jealousy and ambition, you find disharmony and wicked things of every kind being done.

(James 3:16)

QUOTE

We imposed our civilization as a condition of accepting the Gospel. We tried to make you be like us and in so doing we helped to destroy the vision that made you what you were … We ask you to forgive us.

(*An Apology to Native Elders from the United Church of Canada*, 15 August 1986)

FACTFILE

Howard Souster

Howard Souster (born 1919) was training to become a dentist when he heard a missionary talking about his work. At once he changed his training to become a doctor. He offered to serve the Methodist Missionary Society in China – but the Society sent him to Nigeria instead. He worked in Eastern Nigeria, where he carried out over 6000 operations. Now the hospitals are run by the local churches, but Dr Souster helps to recruit staff for them.

The Church has been active in Africa from its earliest days. Scholars think that St Mark founded the Coptic Church in Egypt in the first century. There has been an Orthodox Church in Ethiopia since the fourth century.

When missionaries arrived in Africa from Europe, they brought their own style of Christian worship. They also brought their own type of buildings, dress, music, beliefs and values. They knew nothing about African traditions, nor about African religions that were thousands of years old; neither did they care.

Recently, the Church in Africa has begun to change as African countries have become independent. Many Churches changed the way they expressed their faith. They remained Christian, but began to use African ideas and patterns of worship.

They became the Independent African Churches.

SOME CHARACTERISTICS

The Independent Churches use traditional African dance, music, story-telling, symbols and **rituals**. Some include ancient African ideas about the worship of ancestors. For some, Jesus Christ is 'the light' who sends away evil and darkness. For others he is the 'giver of life' and 'the healer'.

Some of the most popular churches are the 'prophet-healing' Churches. Their leaders are called prophets. They claim to have received a vision from God, who gives them power to heal in his name.

These may seem strange to Christians from Europe. In some ways the Church in Africa needed to change, to give the Church its African character. People felt the missionaries did not just want to convert Africans to Christianity, they wanted to make them into 'black Europeans'. The missionaries had even insisted that African Christians must be baptized with European Christian names. An African name that meant 'God with us' was not acceptable – John or Elijah was!

THE COPTIC CHURCH

The oldest church in the world is probably the Coptic Orthodox Church that St Mark founded in the first century in Egypt.

St Anthony (c.251–356) was a member of the Coptic Church. At the age of twenty, he read the words of Jesus in Matthew's Gospel 'If you want to be perfect, go and sell all you have and give the money to the poor ... then come and follow me'. So he went to live alone in a mountain cave in the desert of Egypt. He spent his time in prayer and study. He found this very hard and was often tempted to give up, but he was determined. In time, some disciples gathered around him. Many others came to him for guidance, for healing and to hear him teach. He persuaded other people living alone, called hermits, to form small communities. This became the first monastery. Monasticism had begun (see unit 35). St Anthony died aged 105 and the monastery he founded is still in use.

The world's first monastery was founded in the desert

Coptic priests and monks

LIFE IN THE DESERT

The bishops of the Coptic Church all come from monasteries. In St Anthony's Monastery, 500 kilometres south of Cairo, the monks get up at 3 a.m. and spend the next five hours praying together. Then they work through the day, usually on the land. They are skilled farmers and can raise crops, even in the desert. Father Dioscorus, one of the monks, explains.

> Many people think we come to the desert to punish ourselves … But it's not true. We come because we love it here. We love the peace, the silence. When you are in love you want to be alone with your lover – you want to sit together in a quiet place and talk, not to be in the midst of a crowd of other people … We come here because, well, we want to be alone with our God. As St Anthony once said, 'Let your heart be silent, then God will speak'.

COPTIC WORSHIP

The Eucharist is central to Coptic worship. Music also plays an important part in worship. People think that many of the chants and hymns date back to the temple music of ancient Egypt.

There have been many martyrs in the Coptic Church. Their relics are thought to be very holy. They may be used in parts of worship. The Coptic Church is still sometimes persecuted today because it exists in the middle of the Muslim world. The desert monasteries still provide refuge for Coptic Christians.

Chapter 2 of St Matthew's Gospel tells how the Holy Family (Jesus and his parents) escaped into Egypt. This is an important event for the Coptic Church. There are many **pilgrimage** sites in the country connected with the Holy Family and the Virgin Mary. Coptic Christians greatly honour the mother of Christ. They believe that she appeared at Zeitoun in Egypt between 1968 and 1970.

The Coptic Church has a long history, but it is very much alive in the modern world. Many of its members are involved in medicine, education and agriculture. The head of the Church is Pope Shenouda III who lives in Cairo. In 1994 the British Orthodox Church became part of the Coptic Orthodox Church.

FACTFILE

John Mbiti (1931–)

John Mbiti was born in Kitui, Kenya. He is a modern African theologian and writer. He says Africa did not need 'imported Christianity', nor the Western style of dress, music and buildings imposed by the early missionaries. He agrees that these missionaries were 'devout, sincere and dedicated men and women' – but they had a negative attitude to existing African religions. Mbiti says the traditional African religions were preparation for Christianity and were searching for the Ultimate.

INTRODUCTION

Today, millions of people follow religions such as Buddhism, Hinduism, Islam, Judaism, Sikhism and others. This is in addition to the millions who are Christian.

In the past there has been conflict among these religions, sometimes with war and bloodshed. Some people believe that their own religion is the only true one, so all others must be false. This narrow-minded attitude has resulted in missionaries from some religions trying to force people to change their own beliefs.

Christians have often been guilty of this, too. They used to think followers of other religions were pagans or heathens. Even today, there are groups of Christians who strongly believe that the only way to God and salvation is through belief in Jesus Christ. People who do not share their belief find this attitude harsh and divisive.

THE RELIGIOUS ANIMAL

Humans are often called 'religious animals'. Only human beings seem to be aware of the spiritual world. In every period of history, in every culture and in every part of the world, people have believed in forces and powers that exist beyond and within this world.

Different cultures may express their beliefs differently. Their rituals, or what they do, may seem very different. But many scholars think that beneath it all they share many similar beliefs.

In the past, travellers saw and recorded the differences. They failed to look for what these religions had in common. They did not take the religions of other people seriously enough to explore and exchange ideas.

There must be peace among the world's religions

GLOBAL VILLAGE

Some people think that we all live in a 'global village'. They say that the world is 'shrinking'. Television, radio and the Internet let us see and hear what is happening on the other side of the world almost as soon as it happens. We can travel across the world in a few hours. This increases our awareness of the peoples of the world, and of their beliefs, ideas, cultures and customs.

As we get to know more about people and their beliefs, we realize their culture is as important to them as ours is to us. In our present time, people from different religions are getting together to talk, listen and learn from each other.

SIMILARITY

Despite the differences in beliefs and practices among religions, there are strange and interesting similarities.

Look at these sayings from the Hindu, Jewish, Muslim and Christian scriptures.

The life, or self, of this whole universe, is the same as that tiny seed from which it came. You are that self.

(Upanishad 6:12:3)

The Lord is near to all who call upon him, to all who call upon him in truth.

(Psalm 145:18)

We are nearer to him than his jugular vein.

(Surah 50:15)

… for behold, the Kingdom of God is within you.

(Luke 17:21)

DIALOGUE

Dialogue means talking together. In the past, Christians believed theirs was the only true religion. They saw other religions as either worthless or, at least, inferior. Now Christian scholars believe that dialogue can help to bring believers together. The aim is not to make all religions the same, but to learn what others have to say.

POINTS OF VIEW

The teachings of Jesus, Muhammad, Lao-Tzu, the Buddha, are all the same. There is only one happiness. There are a thousand … heralds, but only one voice. The voice of God does not come just from the Bible. The essence of love, beauty and holiness does not reside in Christianity … it resides in you and me, in each one of us. This is the one eternal truth. It is the doctrine of the 'Kingdom of Heaven' that we bear within ourselves. Demand more of yourselves. Love and joy and the mysterious things we call happiness are not over here or over there, they are only 'within ourselves'.

(Herman Hesse – twentieth-century writer)

FACTFILE

Definitions

Not everyone has religious beliefs. **Atheists** believe there is no god. **Agnostics** think it is impossible to know if god exists. **Humanists** believe it is important to live for the welfare of others. A humanist may be from any system of beliefs – or none.

33 LIBERATION THEOLOGY

INTRODUCTION

In Central and South America there are rich natural resources. The countries are run by a wealthy ruling class, but most of the people are very poor. In the 1960s a number of Christians, mainly Roman Catholics, started a movement called 'Liberation Theology'.

The members of the movement believe that the Gospels are telling people to stand up and fight against poverty, injustice and the lack of human rights. For instance, Luke's Gospel, says:

> He has chosen me to bring good news to the poor … to proclaim liberty to the captives … and to set free the oppressed.
>
> (Luke 4:18)

> How terrible for you who are rich now; you have had your easy life.
> How terrible for you who are full now: you will go hungry!
>
> (Luke 6:24–5)

At first, the Roman Catholic Church in that part of the world did little to fight injustice. However, many priests took the part of the poor, as Jesus did. They asked:

- 'What should we do, as Christians, when we see how deadly and oppressive the lives of our people are?'

- 'Why is there such poverty among so many, when there are enough resources for everyone?'

BASE CHRISTIAN COMMUNITIES

These are groups of ordinary people who come together to work for change. They want to take action in the world, on behalf of God. Governments and Church leaders often criticize them because they are challenging 'the system'. This system allows torture, killings, corruption and death squads to go hand-in-hand with poverty.

Liberation Theologians say it is not enough to talk about being the Church of the poor. The Church must be a poor Church.

STATE VIOLENCE

In countries such as El Salvador, anybody who stands up against the government risks their life. In 1980 Archbishop Oscar Romero (see unit 16) was shot by assassins while he celebrated mass. On Christmas Eve 1979 he had said:

> We must seek [the child Jesus] among the … children who have gone to bed tonight without eating, among the poor newsboys who will sleep covered with newspapers in doorways.

In 1989, government soldiers went into the university in San Salvador and shot dead six Jesuit priests, their housekeeper and her sixteen-year-old daughter. Many other Church workers, priests and nuns have been imprisoned, tortured and killed. A death squad leaflet said, 'Be a patriot – kill a priest.'

Bodies of Church members killed in Nicaragua

FATHER CAMILO TORRES

This kind of violence still happens in Nicaragua, where the Church sided with the poor. Some Christians saw that peaceful ways did not work, so they took up arms. They felt that governments did not listen to non-violent protest. In Columbia, Father Camilo Torres (1929–66) became a freedom fighter. He was killed in a gun battle with government forces. He wrote:

> The basic thing … is loving one's neighbour. For this love to be true it has to be effective … We must take power [and] give it to the poor majority. The revolution can be peaceful, only if the minorities do not offer violent resistance.

Most Liberation Theologians believe that violence is wrong. But where governments use extreme violence against poor people, Camillo Torres said: 'the Catholic who is not revolutionary is living in mortal sin'.

LIBERATION THEOLOGY IN BRITAIN…

Liberation Theology has spread to Britain and other parts of the world. Some bishops now speak out against government policies which may hurt the poor. For instance, David Sheppard, former Anglican Bishop of Liverpool, wrote an important book, *Bias to the Poor*. In it he wrote about high unemployment, inner-city problems, bad housing and lack of government help for the poor.

…AND SOUTH AFRICA

In South Africa, Christians such as Desmond Tutu, Trevor Huddleston and Alan Boesak were inspired by Liberation Theology. They wanted to liberate black South Africans from the unfair system of *apartheid*. In 1994 the first multi-racial elections took place. The work of brave Christians like these helped to bring apartheid to an end.

POINTS OF VIEW

- This theology … tries to be part of the process through which the world is transformed.

(Gustavo Guttierez – Liberation theologian)

- When I give food to the poor, they call me a saint. When I ask why the poor have no food, they call me a communist.

(Helder Camara – Brazilian Bishop)

- The cry of the poor is for justice not charity. Dignity is as important as bread.

(Asian Ecumenical Conference)

FACTFILE

David Sheppard (1929–)

David Sheppard was born in 1929. He became an outstanding cricketer. A well-known sports writer described him as 'one of the sporting heroes of his generation'. While he enjoyed his sport, he also thought deeply about the important work which he felt God was calling him to do. He became an Anglican priest and worked mainly in the poorer areas of London's docklands. He still played cricket and earned 22 caps for his country. While he was Bishop of Liverpool, he was able to use his influence to try to improve conditions for poor people, by bringing them to the attention of the government.

Feminist theology is a way of talking about God from a woman's point of view. Dr Melissa Raphael teaches and writes about this subject. In this unit we look at her main ideas.

WOMEN'S VIEWPOINTS

It is not simply a question of women's liberation or sexual equality. We need a new perspective on the way we look at women and men, nature and God.

Feminist theologians do not say that God is a woman! They are not just insisting that women should be allowed to be priests. They are not even saying women shouldn't help to raise money for charity, make tea, clean the brass or arrange flowers in Church.

What they *are* saying, is that we need to re-think the language we use about God. We are so used to hearing God referred to as 'he' that we don't even notice that females get left out. This is because most theology has been written by men, for men and about men. When women are mentioned, they seem to be either saintly mothers (like Mary, who was a virgin) or temptresses like Eve.

MASCULINE LANGUAGE

Tertullian (c.160–215), one of the Church Fathers, called women 'the devil's gateway'. Nowadays theologians are less harsh. But the idea of 'God the Father' who became incarnate as 'Jesus the Son' had the effect of seeming to glorify men and damage women's self-esteem. It works like this:

The Bible and Christian writers nearly always use masculine words for God, such as Father, King, Shepherd and Lord. This means that women, half the human race, are left out of ideas about God. This allows human kings and fathers to rule on behalf of God, and to claim the right to speak on any topic on behalf of everyone. This silences women.

There are few records of what women think or experience of God. Many women feel less than human and certainly less than divine.

SIN

Feminist theologians say that male ideas of ruling 'from above' also influence the way we think about sin. It is as though sin was simply 'disobeying orders'. Feminists argue that sin is about 'wrong relationships'. Sin is about exploiting people and the earth's resources. They feel that God is present in all creation and that therefore all life is sacred. Creation must be respected because it comes from God.

If we learn to respect all creation, this will help to overcome racism, national and religious hatred, and destruction of the natural environment.

PATRIARCHY

The problem arose mainly because the Church took on ancient Greek and Mediaeval patriarchal attitudes. Patriarchy means 'rule by the fathers' (see unit 67). We must replace this kind of thinking by a more caring, unisex viewpoint. We could do this by using more inclusive language. We could talk of motherhood as well as fatherhood, or use more abstract names for God such as the *Holy One*.

Most Christians today think that it is wrong to talk of God in female terms because Jesus did not. But many go much further. They believe that there is a chain of command which begins with God at the top, down through Jesus, to husbands and finally to wives and children at the bottom. Men keep their power by saying that the husband must be head of the family (and therefore of society) because Eve – a woman – brought sin into the world. As a result all women have to be punished by having periods ('the curse'), painful childbirth and submitting to their husbands. This teaching is

sed on Genesis 3:16; 1 Timothy 2:12–16;
hesians 5:22–3 and 1 Corinthians 11:3.

HE BIBLE

ristian feminists still turn to the Bible for
spiration. This is because some of the
ophets, Jesus himself, and the role of
omen in the early Church, seem to pinpoint
e kind of world that feminism is working
r. But they feel that in some parts the Bible
pports the patriarchal view, and these parts
not reveal God in a true sense. They use
e Bible carefully and look for 'woman-
ntred' teachings.

EMINISTS IN THE PAST

cently, feminist writings from the past have
nerged. For example, in 1373 Mother
lian of Norwich wrote, *'Jesus Christ who
turns good for evil is our true Mother. We
ve our being from him, the ground and
urce of all motherhood.'*

A seventeenth-century Roman Catholic priest
wrote:

> Did the woman say
> when she held him for the first time
> in the dark of a stable,
> after the pain and the bleeding and the
>   crying
> 'This is my body, this is my blood'?

> Did the woman say
> when she held him for the last time
> in the dark on a hilltop,
> after the pain and the bleeding
>   and the dying
> 'This is my body, this is my blood'?

> Well that she said it to him then,
> for dry old men,
> brocaded robes belying barrenness,
> ordain that she not say it for him now.

lam   *Eve*

FACTFILE

Attitudes to women in the Gospels

In Luke's Gospel we read about Jesus'
attitude towards Mary of Magdala.
'You see this woman? I came to your
house: you gave me no water for my
feet; but this woman has made my
feet wet with her tears and dried them
with her hair. You did not welcome me
with a kiss; but she has not stopped
kissing my feet since I came in. You
provided no olive-oil for my head; but
she has covered my feet with perfume.
I tell you then the great love she has
shown proves that her many sins have
been forgiven ...' Read the rest of this
story in Luke 7:36–50.

A monk can be happy without worldly success

Monasticism is the way of life in which people live in separate communities, obeying religious vows they have taken. Men who do this are called monks or brothers. They live in monasteries. Women are nuns or sisters. They live in convents.

EARLY MONASTERIES

The first monastery was begun in Egypt in the fourth century by St Anthony (see unit 31). By about 530 CE an Italian, called Benedict, began a monastery in Europe. His rules for the monastic life are called the Rule of St Benedict. St Benedict described the monastery as 'a school of the service of the Lord'.

Other monastic orders were soon set up. In 1209 St Francis formed the Franciscan Order. His brothers lived a life of poverty, like Jesus.

At about the same time Dominic, a Spanish priest, set up the Dominican Order. His brothers were travelling preachers, but they did not live in poverty like the Franciscans.

MONASTICISM TODAY

Men and women who become monks or nuns take vows of poverty, chastity and obedience. They fill their lives with prayer, reading, meditation, worship and work. The work may be manual labour, on the land, o teaching, or caring for the sick.

People who join religious communities promise to give their whole lives to serving God and developing their spiritual nature. It not an escape from the world! They live clos to each other and have to face all the usual problems of personal relationships. They hav to work hard, both at their daily jobs and on themselves, to develop and grow.

Trappists monks take a vow of silence as we as their other vows. Thomas Merton (1915–68) was a famous Trappist monk. He wrote many influential books about civil rights and nuclear disarmament.

> This is an age … which calls for the special searching and questioning which are the work of the monk in his meditation and prayer … the monk abandons the world only in order to listen more intently to the deepest and most neglected voices that proceed from its inner depths.
>
> (Thomas Merton, *Contemplative Prayer*

The Rule of St Francis

This is the Rule and way of life of the brothers of mine: to observe the holy Gospel of our Lord Jesus Christ, living in obedience, without personal possessions and in chastity.

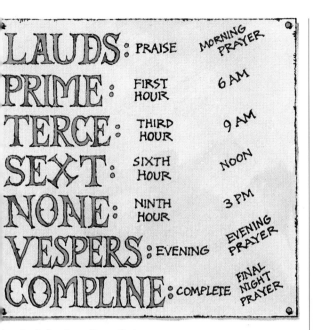

LAUDS : PRAISE		MORNING PRAYER
PRIME : FIRST HOUR		6 AM
TERCE : THIRD HOUR		9 AM
SEXT : SIXTH HOUR		NOON
NONE : NINTH HOUR		3 PM
VESPERS : EVENING		EVENING PRAYER
COMPLINE : COMPLETE		FINAL NIGHT PRAYER

typical day in a Benedictine monastery

Some of Benedict's Rules

Above all, let not the evil of grumbling appear, on any account, by the least sign or word whatever.

Let the monks sleep clothed girdled with belts or cords ... And thus let the monks be always ready; when the signal is given, let them rise without delay.

Let all guests who arrive be received like Christ, for he is going to say 'I came as a guest and you received me.'

REFLECTIONS

When I was sixteen I realized that I had to be a nun. There was no sudden flash: it was rather as if the truth had been there in my mind for a long time. I believe we are chosen ...

(Dame Maria Boulding)

When people ask me why I became a monk, I feel very like the engaged couple who are asked why they have fallen in love. We don't really know.

(Dom Leonard Vickers)

The monk is there to show that one can be perfectly happy without depending on any worldly success or achievement. The monk bears witness to the fact that the happiness of the Christian life does not depend on the promises of this world.

(Thomas Merton, *Contemplation in a World of Action*)

FACTFILE

The Poor Clares

St Francis gave up riches and luxury to follow a life of poverty to serve Jesus Christ. In his town of Assisi a young girl, Clare, who was also from a rich and noble family, decided to live the strict life of a nun.

She wanted to live as Francis did, with no possessions of her own. Soon a group of women who thought the same joined her. It was the beginning of the order of nuns now known as the Poor Clares. They had a very hard life indeed – but they were happy believing this helped them to serve God. Today the Poor Clares still lead a life of prayer and hard work, with strict fasting. They wear dark brown habits and cloth sandals on bare feet.

St Francis of Assisi in meditation

People in religious communities have many different kinds of work to do (see unit 35). One important part of life for monks and nuns is contemplation. This may mean thinking deeply and quietly about the meaning of life, or trying to stop all thoughts about anything else, to allow silence and inner peace to take over. Contemplation is a spiritual and mystical aspect of life (see unit 14).

Here are some short profiles of the lives of two famous contemplatives.

Basil the Great, 330–79 CE

Basil is greatly honoured in the Greek Orthodox Church. He gave up a successful life as a teacher and became a hermit. Later, with a friend called Gregory, he set up a monastery. He also built hostels for the poor and hospitals for the sick near the monastery. His Rules were originally intended for monks, but they are relevant for Christians today. For example:

> If a man says he finds the teaching of holy scripture sufficient to correct his character, he makes himself like a man who learns the theory of building but never practises the art … The Lord Jesus … was not content with teaching the word only … but he girded himself and washed the feet of his disciples in person. Whose feet will you wash? For whom will you care?

Teresa of Avila , 1515–82 CE

St Teresa is much loved and respected in the Roman Catholic Church for her teaching on true spirituality. At the age of twenty she became a Carmelite nun. She wrote many books on spirituality which still inspire Christians today. In her book *Life* she describes some of her spiritual experiences.

> I used unexpectedly to experience a consciousness of the presence of God … This was in some sense a vision: I believe it is called mystical theology. The soul is suspended in such a way that it seems to be completely outside itself. The will leaves: the memory, I think, is almost lost: while the understanding, I believe, though not lost does not reason – I mean that it does not work, but is amazed at the extent of all it can understand.

fter her death, these words were found
ritten on a card. They are sometimes called
t Teresa's bookmark':

Let nothing disturb you;
Let nothing dismay you;
All things pass;
God never changes.
Patience attains
All that it strives for.
He who has God
Finds he lacks nothing;
God alone suffices.

REFLECTION

Brother David is a modern Benedictine monk. Here he talks about the contemplative life, which he describes as 'spiritual work'. He says that people today are no longer in touch with their roots. He calls this 'uprootedness'.

Think for instance, of the uprootedness that comes as a by-product of mobility. Now, it is very good that we can move quickly and easily from place to place. But there are families in the United States who move more than twenty times while their children are growing up. Think of our uprootedness from our families. There are many people who have had little or no contact with their grandparents …

Or think of our uprootedness from the earth. Do you know the garden from which your fruits and vegetables come?

How many people in the world know the well from which their water comes? … This used to be rather important.

He asks whether we really know ourselves as body-spirits. He even wonders whether we are rooted in time.

Most of the time, 48 per cent of us is clinging to the past, 51 per cent is stretching out towards the future and 1 per cent is left to be present where we are at the moment. So [even our time is] just passing us by while we are busy with nostalgic memories or impatient fantasies.

The spiritual work of our time is the task of making alive, of rerooting – because if something is cut off from its roots it will sooner or later die. That's the image of flesh – something that's cut off from its life, its roots.

KEY WORD

Worship – to show great respect for God, especially in a religious service; actions that show feelings of **adoration** (great love)

For Christians, worship is a way of expressing what they believe about Jesus Christ. It is important for them to meet regularly with other believers to worship together. At other times they may worship on their own or with their families. Sunday is the holy day for Christians. They usually gather for worship in a church building. In most Christian groups, members of the congregation take part in the worship. Many denominations have full-time clergy (see unit 44) who run the churches and lead worship.

DIFFERENCES OF STYLE

Liturgical or formal worship

Liturgy is a Greek word meaning public worship. In this style of worship, all the actions follow a set pattern. Liturgical worship is often formal, elaborate and colourful. Roman Catholic, Orthodox and some Anglican Churches worship in this way. They express their beliefs, using symbolic acts and special objects. These Churches place a great value on the sacraments (see unit 41).

Non-liturgical worship

The worship in many Protestant Churches avoids set rituals and symbolic actions. These Christians give more importance to Bible readings, prayers, hymns and sermons. The least formal style of worship is practised by the Society of Friends (see unit 42).

Why Christians worship

The different styles of worship show that different Christians emphasize different aspects of worship. Those who prefer liturgical worship emphasize outward signs and symbols which express deep religious and spiritual feelings. Those who use the les formal styles place more importance on the 'Word of God', and not ritual actions.

For Christians, acts of worship:

- enable them to express their faith
- inspire and strengthen them for their dail lives
- enable them to give praise and thanks to God, and show their love, wonder, commitment and repentance.

All this can be expressed through art, music clapping, communion, ringing bells, prayers kissing icons, burning incense, lighting candles, Bible readings, making the sign of the cross, story-telling, wearing special clothes and giving money.

Some Christians take their ideas of worship into their everyday lives, and perform every task as an act of service to God. Whether gardening or cooking, studying or teaching, everything is done as part of daily worship.

Acts of worship enable Christians to express their faith

FACTFILE

Pliny's report

In about 112 CE a Roman official called Pliny reported on a new religion: '… on an appointed day they used to meet before daybreak and to recite a hymn to Christ … and to bind themselves by an oath … After this ceremony it was their custom to meet again to take food …' He added that the new religion had spread 'to cities, villages and country districts as well.'

REFLECTION

Bishop Simon Barrington-Ward tries to explain how, at emotional times in our lives, we may give thanks together without prompting.

'Everyone suddenly burst out singing
And I was filled with such delight
As prisoned birds must find in freedom
Winging wildly across the white
Orchard and dark green fields; on; on;
   and out of sight.
Everyone's voice was suddenly lifted
And beauty came like the setting sun.
My heart was shaken with tears, and
   horror
Drifted away … O but everyone
Was a bird and the song was wordless
The singing will never be done.'

Siegfried Sassoon's famous poem (above) for Armistice Day 1918 celebrated the end of four years of war. Previously he had described terrible glimpses of life in the trenches. Now, in one moment, the cloud parted. A long-dreamed-of breakthrough had come.

The Bishop goes on to ask, 'Can you imagine the scene?' He describes the way the music seems to rise up and take over the singers. Most of us have known moments like that, when something sudden and unexpected happens. It may be a reunion or a farewell party. Someone starts to sing and others join in. The crowd begins to sway to the music.

They put their arms round each other's shoulders perhaps. Then it happens. Your inner feeling and the world round you and the people with you all flow together …

You feel the people are totally united. You feel as though the Spirit is:

… carrying you upward, forward, out of yourself … A movement like that seems to be a kind of harvest festival … We offer ourselves. The past is gathered in with the present. All that we have, all that we are, is taken up … ready to be changed, ready to be poured out: expended; wholly given. Our only thought is an inexpressible thankfulness and gladness.
'Then was our mouth filled with laughter, And our tongue with singing …'
At such times a door seems to open in the surface of life and lead us deeper … into that greater wholeness which lies beyond our so-called 'everyday' life.

'We all have the need to worship …'

REFLECTION

We all have the need to worship – to worship something or someone greater than ourselves, to whom we wish to dedicate our whole lives. Sometimes they say we all have a God-shaped space inside us and only God can fill it. This means that we are created by God, we are created like God, and we are created for God. … and nothing less than God can really ever satisfy our hunger for God.

Others try to worship things that are less than God – it may be money, or ambition, or drugs or sex. In the end they find out that they are worthless idols. To worship means to give due worth to someone or something. We give worth to God. Worship is absolutely central to our faith where God comes first, always. We bow before His infinite majesty and holiness, trembling with awe at his unapproachable light and radiance. Many times we feel that words are utterly inadequate, so we keep a deep silence in the holy presence. But true Christian worship can never let us be indifferent to the needs of others, to the cries of the hungry, of the naked and the homeless, of the sick and the prisoner, of the oppressed and the disadvantaged.

True Christian worship includes the love of God and the love of neighbour … or your Christianity is false. We are Christian not only in church on Sunday. Our Christianity is not something we put on like our Sunday best. It is for every day. We must worship our God for ever and ever, and serve Him by serving our neighbour today and always.

(Archbishop Desmond Tutu, *Hope and Suffering*)

Religion has three important features. These are doctrine (statements about beliefs), deeds and worship. The three go together. For Christians, worship is linked to what they believe and what they do. The Reflection opposite shows how true worship includes 'serving our neighbour'.

CHRISTIAN BELIEF

As we have seen in previous units, Christians believe that above and beyond this physical world there is another reality. They use the word **transcendent** to describe this other reality. Transcendent means 'beyond normal limits'.

The Christian writer Francis Thompson (1859–1907) connects the physical world and the transcendent world:

O World Invisible, we view thee,
O World Intangible, we touch thee,
O World Unknowable, we know thee,
Inapprehensible, we clutch thee.

(Francis Thompson, 'The Kingdom of God')

For Christians, there are ways of making contact with this 'other' reality. For example:

- listening to, and taking part in great music
- reading holy scriptures
- expressing transcendent ideas in beautiful buildings
- by prayer, contemplation, silence and deep thought.

CHRISTIAN DEEDS

Christian belief cannot be separated from Christian worship. In their lives, Christians try to act out of love, as followers of Jesus Christ. However, they believe that they need God's help – grace (see unit 9) – to do this. Christians believe that worship helps them to get near to God, who gives them grace to face up to all life's problems and challenges.

QUOTE

The worship of God is not a rule of safety – it is an adventure of the spirit …

(A. N. Whitehead – scholar)

KEY IDEAS

Two aspects of Christian worship are:

- offering – this is all that goes out from the worshipper, e.g. praise, adoration (great love)
- receiving – this is all that comes back, e.g. fellowship, inspiration, strength.

FACTFILE

How to pray

Jesus taught his followers to pray privately and sincerely. He said, 'When you pray, do not be like the hypocrites! They love to stand up and pray in the houses of worship and on the street corners so that everyone will see them … But when you pray, go to your room, close the door, and pray to your Father, who is unseen. And your Father, who sees what you do in private, will reward you.' (Matthew 6:5–6).

Ely Cathedral

Chiu Chiu Calama, Chile

Most local Christian groups worship in special buildings. In this unit we look at the many types of buildings and the way differences have come about because of the different beliefs and practices of the various groups.

Some Christian groups do not think that the building is important. They find that too much emphasis on material things, such as church buildings, gets in the way of their faith. Others, like Quakers, may meet in a very simple building, or a room that they rent in a school.

Many other Christians think of their places of worship as sacred or holy. The holy place helps them to sense the presence of God in a special way, and to concentrate on their worship.

FEATURES OF PLACES OF WORSHIP

- Many cathedrals and churches are beautifully decorated and furnished. This gives believers a sense of God's glory.

- The most holy part of Anglican and Roman Catholic churches is the **altar**, or holy table. Many Christians feel this is the place where Jesus' presence can be felt most deeply during the Eucharist.

- If someone preaches in a service, then they preach from a raised platform. This is the **pulpit**. It may be made of wood or stone and it usually has steps to reach it. In Methodist churches the pulpit may be more prominent than the altar, because of the greater importance they give to the spoken word (see diagram 1).

Many churches and cathedrals have tall spires pointing to the sky. Others may have square towers. Some churches have bell towers and the bells are rung at special times.

Stained-glass windows are a feature in many churches and cathedrals. They may tell a story or express a symbol of belief.

Traditional churches have a cruciform (cross-shaped) plan (see diagram 2). The seats are arranged so that the people face east (where the sun rises). This symbolizes the resurrection of Jesus.

Baptists believe that people should be baptized only when they are old enough to understand what they are promising. For them the **baptistry**, or pool for baptizing members, is very important. It is often a central feature of Baptist churches.

In other churches there is a **font** (a large stone bowl) which contains water for baptism. This may be near the church entrance, because baptism means entering the Church.

In some churches there are wooden booths or confessionals. These are where a person may confess their sins to a priest in private.

- In some churches there is a small chapel, dedicated to the Virgin Mary, containing a statue of her. This is called the Lady Chapel.

FACTFILE

The first meeting places

For the first century or so, Christians did not have special buildings in which to worship. They met in houses or on hillsides. The Eucharist was usually celebrated in a private house. In the east, the dining-room was often used. In Rome, where people lived in apartments, the largest room available would be used. In time, people began to donate houses to the Church and these were specially adapted for worship. One house named *Dura Europos* had two rooms knocked into one, a special entrance and a baptistry, complete with font and wall decorations.

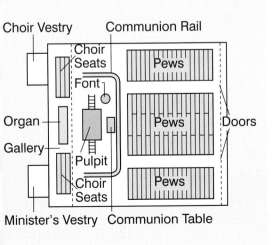

Diagram 1: Plan of a Methodist church

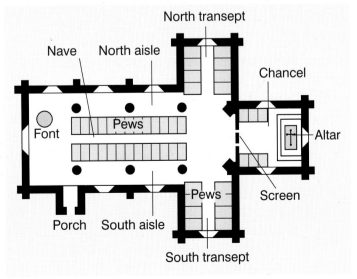

Diagram 2: Plan of a cruciform church

INTRODUCTION

In this unit we look at two places of Christian worship. They are two of the most beautiful buildings in the world. Both are in France, and were built in about the twelfth century. They are the Gothic cathedrals of Chartres and Notre-Dame.

These wonderful buildings were built at a time of great cruelty. The Roman Catholic Church was hunting down and murdering heretics (people who didn't agree with its teachings). The Crusades, carried out in the name of God, caused death and suffering in Europe and Palestine. Yet, despite this, the spires of Chartres and Notre-Dame reach up to the heavens, to remind women and men of God's presence on earth.

MYSTERIOUS ORIGINS

The history of these two wonderful buildings is very mysterious. No one is sure who built them. At the time there were Schools of Builders, but very little is actually known about these schools and the men and women in them. The cathedrals may be their work. Certainly the Roman Catholic Church did not build them.

Some scholars think that an Order of Knights planned and built the cathedrals. They were the Knights Templar. They followed the orders of Bernard of Clairvaux, who founded the Cistercian Order of Monks. They gave up all their worldly possessions and spent ten years in the Holy Land (Palestine). During that time they searched for certain secrets among the ancient ruins of Solomon's Temple. When they returned, they brought with them knowledge about astronomy, architecture, mathematics, stone-masonry, glass-making, psychology and physiology. One theory is that they put their knowledge into practice by building the cathedrals – but nobody knows for sure!

The rose window, Notre-Dame, Paris

PILGRIMS

Many **pilgrims** visit both cathedrals to worship and pray to the Virgin Mary. Many have written about how the power of the buildings themselves can 'refresh the soul' of visitors.

When the first Christians arrived in France in the third century CE they discovered a carving of a Virgin with child, blackened with age, at an ancient Druid shrine in Chartres. The astonished Christians believed that the Druids had received a vision of the Virgin many years before the birth of Christ. They built the first church on this site. Afterwards five more were built. Five of these six churches were destroyed by fire.

REFLECTION

Peter Ouspensky wrote a book called *A New Model of the Universe*. He writes about the strange thoughts that came to him when he looked out over the city of Paris from the tower of Notre-Dame.

A small medieval town surrounded by fields, vineyards and woods. A growing Paris which several times outgrew its walls … And the people, forever going somewhere past these towers, forever hurrying somewhere, and always remaining where they were, seeing nothing, noticing nothing, always the same people. And the towers always the same, with the same gargoyles looking on at this town, which is for ever changing, for ever disappearing and yet always remaining the same.

Here two lines in the life of humanity are clearly seen. One is the line of life of those people below; and the other, the line of the life of those who built Notre-Dame. And looking down from those towers you feel that the real history … is the history of the people who built Notre-Dame and not that of those below … these are two quite different histories.

One history passes by in full view … the history of crime, for if there were no crimes there would be no history. All the most important turning points and stages of this history are marked by crimes: murders, acts of violence, robberies, wars, rebellions, massacres, tortures, executions …

This is one history …

The other history is the history which is known to very few. … what is created by this hidden history exists long afterwards, sometimes for many centuries, as does Notre-Dame … I was wandering about the town for the last time. It was already growing light and the air was becoming cold … The huge massive towers stood as though on alert. But I already understood their secret. … that there is another history apart from the history of crimes, and that there is another thought, which created Notre-Dame and its figures.

(Peter Ouspensky, *A New Model of the Universe*)

Notre-Dame Cathedral, Paris

FACTFILE

Churches dedicated to Mary

Notre-Dame is one of the many churches throughout the world that are dedicated to Mary, Mother of Christ. *Notre-Dame* means 'Our Lady'.

INTRODUCTION

The Christian scholar St Augustine (354–430 CE) said that a sacrament was 'the visible form of an invisible grace'.

A sacrament is a special Christian celebration. There are symbolic actions or objects for each of the sacraments. They represent spiritual or invisible things. For example, the bread and wine of the Eucharist represent or symbolize the body and blood of Jesus Christ.

The Roman Catholic and Orthodox Churches have seven sacraments. These are listed below. Most Protestant Churches accept only the first two, the Eucharist and baptism. Some Christians, including the Society of Friends, may not use any sacraments at all.

THE SEVEN SACRAMENTS

- **The Eucharist** or Holy Communion (see unit 43) – This central act of worship recalls the death and resurrection of Jesus. It repeats the words and actions of Jesus at the Last Supper (see Mark 14:17–25).

- **Baptism** (see unit 55) – In this ceremony a child or adult is 'washed clean' of sin to begin a new life with God.

- **Confirmation** (see unit 55) – This is when a baptized person becomes a full member of the Church. The person confirms the promises made by godparents, at his or her baptism.

- **Marriage** (see units 56 and 57) – In this sacrament the man and woman promise themselves to each other for life.

- **Penance** – This is sometimes called confession. People confess their sins to a priest. They express their sincere sorrow, and promise to try not to sin again. The priest forgives the sinner in God's name. This enables the person to return to God and the Church. Roman Catholics must

Holy Communion in an Anglican church

confess their sins at least once a year, but the Church encourages people to confess more often than this.

- **Ordination** (see unit 44) – This is when people are made deacons, priests or bishops. Bishops themselves usually take charge of ordination services. Part of the ceremony includes the 'laying on of hands'.

- **Anointing the sick** – When people are very ill or very old, a priest may anoint them with oil that has been blessed. This is a sign of healing. In the Greek Orthodox Church, this anointing is performed every year in church for the whole congregation. It takes place on the evening of Holy Wednesday (the Wednesday before Good Friday).

SACRAMENTS AND THE CHURCH

For Christians, a sacrament must be carried out in the church by the appointed leader. Otherwise it does not mean anything. It must be performed by recognized ministers acting for and on behalf of the Church. This is especially important for most Orthodox, Roman Catholic and Protestant Christians.

Christians agree that being a member of a Church community is an important part of their Christian life. They feel that Christ continues his work of salvation through the

Church (see unit 9). A sacrament is not only a visible form of God's grace. Sacraments allow individuals to join in worship with the wider Christian community. The Christian then feels part of the community and shares with others the gift of salvation. The sacraments can be thought of as continual reminders of Christian salvation.

The Churches have not always agreed about the meaning of the sacraments. The most bitter arguments involved the Eucharist (also called Holy Communion, the Lord's Supper or Mass, see unit 43). The Roman Catholic Church taught that the bread and wine of the sacrament became miraculously changed into Christ's actual body and blood during Mass. This was the doctrine of **transubstantiation**. Protestant Christians could not accept this. However, they did agree that Christ was, in some way, present in the Lord's Supper, for those who had faith.

Another major difference is that, while Roman Catholics claimed there were seven sacraments, most Protestants accepted only two. These were the two recorded in the Gospels, in which Christ himself took part (baptism and the Lord's Supper). However, Lutherans accepted the sacrament of penance. In more recent times, many Anglicans have accepted penance, confirmation, matrimony, unction (anointing) and holy orders (ordination). They agree that these five are 'sacred signs' but do not agree that they are as important as baptism and the Eucharist.

The sacraments are powerful experiences for members of the Churches. They are part of the mystery of the Church. Christians believe these mysteries show the Holy Spirit at work.

QUOTE

The Spiritual Presence cannot be received without a sacramental element, however hidden the latter might be.

(Paul Tillich – modern theologian)

FACTFILE

The *Didache*

A very early document called the *Didache* (Greek for teaching) gave the first Church groups guidance about worship. Many of the instructions sound very modern, for example:

… concerning baptism, baptize in this way … baptize in the name of the Father and of the Son and of the Holy Spirit, in running water. But if you do not have running water, baptize in other water; and if you cannot in cold, then in warm. If you have neither, pour water on the head in the name of the Father and of the Son and of the Holy Spirit. Before the baptism let the baptizer and the baptized fast …

THE EASTERN ORTHODOX CHURCH

Icons (see unit 24) are used in Orthodox Churches. They are religious pictures of Jesus or of saints, such as Peter or Mary, the mother of Jesus. These pictures remind Christians that when they worship God they are joining with the saints in heaven.

All Orthodox churches have a screen dividing the main part of the church from the inner sanctuary (the most holy place). This screen is called an *iconostasis*, which means 'place of pictures'. It is usually covered with icons. The screen symbolizes the separation between heaven and earth, between God and people. It has doors which the priest opens at certain moments during the Eucharist to reveal the altar. The doors are opened to remind worshippers that God has ended the separation, by his gift of Jesus Christ.

Another important feature of worship in Orthodox churches is the use of symbolic actions. Each worshipper, on arriving at the church, buys a small candle. The candles are lit and then placed on a stand in front of an icon.

There are no pews or chairs in Orthodox churches. The worshippers stand in groups, then they kneel, or bow at the knee (**genuflect**), or touch the ground with their foreheads during parts of the service. All these movements have symbolic meaning. For example, touching their foreheads to the ground shows submission to God.

THE RELIGIOUS SOCIETY OF FRIENDS (QUAKERS)

The main features of Quaker meetings are stillness and silence. A Quaker meeting begins when the first Friend (the official name for a Quaker) arrives. The Friend enters the room, sits down and waits in

A Society of Friends' meeting for worship

silence, as others arrive, to be aware of God's presence. Gradually the silence deepens. Quakers aim to find a sense of communion with God and with others. When they reach this stage, the Quakers call it a 'gathered meeting'.

A meeting may continue in silence for an hour. Usually, however, a Friend will stand up and speak. They may talk about the life and teaching of Jesus, or about events in the news. They may offer a prayer in their own words. This is called 'vocal ministry'. Anyone – adult or child – may feel that God's spirit is moving them to speak.

After an hour the meeting ends when the elders shake hands. Then everyone may join in, shaking hands with people near to them.

Quaker worship is very simple, with very few aids. The meeting room is plain, with chairs arranged in a square or circle, sometimes round a table.

Quakers do have Quaker Meeting Houses for convenience, but they can meet almost anywhere. They do not think they need a special place. They do not have ordained priests, because they believe that everyone is a priest. They believe it is important to serve God in everyday life and that God's grace can be found anywhere. They do not have sacraments such as the Eucharist, but say that every meal and every meeting can be a time for thanksgiving, remembrance, celebration and fellowship.

THE ROMAN CATHOLIC CHURCH

In a Roman Catholic church you may see stained-glass windows showing the life of Jesus or the saints. There will be pictures of the Stations of the Cross (which tell the story of Jesus carrying his cross) and statues of angels, saints or the Virgin Mary. These are to remind worshippers of God's glory. The main features include the altar and a font for baptisms.

The Mass (see unit 43) is served at the altar. There are Daily Masses and High Masses. These are solemn events when the choir and congregation sing praises to God. Incense is burnt, giving off a sweet-smelling smoke. This is a symbol of holiness. It may be waved towards the altar, the priests and the congregation. A **tabernacle** is fixed on the wall. This is a small metal box that contains a few pieces of **consecrated** bread, called the host. This represents the presence of Christ in the church. Many **lay** (ordinary) people share in the ministry, as readers, servers of the Mass and those who take communion to the sick.

THE UNITED REFORMED CHURCH

In 1972 the Congregational and Presbyterian Churches joined together to form the United Reformed Church (URC). Each congregation is independent and chooses its own minister. The communion table is the focal point in the church, as the Lord's Supper is the most important part of worship. On the communion table there is an empty cross. This symbolizes Jesus' resurrection. There is a font for baptisms. Services include readings from the Bible, a sermon, prayers and hymns. Christians think of hymns as a way of expressing prayer and praise to God.

FACTFILE

William Penn, 1644–1718

William Penn became a Quaker in 1665. He was imprisoned for his faith in 1669. On his release he founded a Quaker colony in America – Pennsylvania.

43 THE EUCHARIST

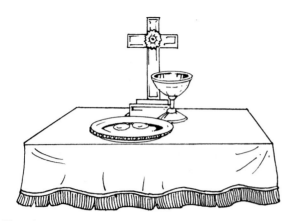

The altar is set for Holy Communion

For many Christians the Eucharist is the most important act of worship. The Eucharist takes its name from a Greek word meaning 'thanksgiving'. The Eucharist recalls Jesus' last meal with his disciples.

> … the Lord Jesus, on the night he was betrayed, took a piece of bread, gave thanks to God, broke it, and said, 'This is my body, which is for you. Do this in memory of me.' In the same way, after the supper he took the cup and said, 'This cup is God's new covenant, sealed with my blood. Whenever you drink it, do so in memory of me.'
>
> (I Corinthians 11:23–5)

The many different names for this great act of Christian thanksgiving include:

- Breaking of bread
- Eucharist
- Lord's Supper
- Mass
- Holy or Sacred Liturgy
- Holy Communion.

Christians may disagree about what Jesus meant when he said the bread was his body and the wine his blood. But they agree that Jesus died on the cross for all human beings. By taking part in the meal, Christians feel they are obeying Jesus' command to do this in remembrance of him.

CELEBRATING THE EUCHARIST

Nearly all Churches celebrate the Eucharist in a similar way, though there may be some differences.

- **The ministry of the Word** – This is the first part of the service. It includes prayers, Bible readings, hymns, acts of confession and perhaps a sermon.

The second part of the service is the celebration of the Eucharist itself:

- **The offering of bread and wine** – Worshippers are reminded how the Eucharist began and the bread and wine are put on the altar or table.

- **The Eucharistic Prayer** or **Great Thanksgiving** – Below is an example of the prayer.

> It is indeed right,
> it is our duty and our joy,
> at all times and in all places
> to give you thanks and praise,
> holy Father, heavenly King,
> Almighty and eternal God,
> Through Jesus Christ your only Son our Lord.

- **The breaking of the bread** – The bread and wine are blessed by the priest or minister. The words said by Jesus at the Last Supper, from the Gospels, may be read out. During the reading, members of the congregation may cross themselves or bow or genuflect. There may be incense round the altar or there may be ringing of bells. The minister may lift up the bread and the wine.

Some congregations greet each other with the 'sign of peace'. They shake hands or embrace those nearest them. This represents unity.

The sharing of the bread and wine – In Orthodox churches, the priest dips a piece of bread in the wine and gives it to members of the the congregation, using a long spoon. In Anglican churches the congregation receives the bread, kneeling at the altar. Each member sips wine from the same **chalice** or cup. In Baptist and some other Protestant Churches, the people take wine from their own little cups that are handed round by the church leaders, or they may stand round the altar or gather in small groups.

- **The dismissal** – After sharing the bread and wine there is a 'dismissal' which may include prayers, a hymn or a blessing. The congregation are then sent out 'to love and serve the Lord'.

In Roman Catholic churches Mass takes place daily. In some Protestant churches the Eucharist may take place once a month. In some churches only those who have been confirmed (see unit 55) are allowed to receive Communion, while other churches have no such rule.

REFLECTIONS

When we receive Communion, I believe that God reaches out to us on the most primitive and simple level. A babe can receive … and with it be reached by God.

(The Most Reverend Metropolitan Anthony of Sourozh, head of the Russian Orthodox Church in Britain)

I cannot do without Mass. If I can see Jesus in the appearance of bread then I will be able to see him in the broken bodies of the poor. He has said, 'I am the Living Bread.'

(Mother Teresa)

I believe that I receive Christ, not because he is in the bread and wine but because he is in the heart of those who receive the bread and wine believingly.

(Reverend John Stott)

'The bread and wine are distributed to the worshippers on conditions of absolute and complete equality. There is no … priority of duke over dustman, it is an act of total sharing and it is in this … that the life of Christ himself is shared.'

(Reverend S. Evans)

FACTFILE

The Eucharistic meal

The Eucharist was one of the earliest sacraments defined by the early Church. Since those early days it has remained almost unchanged. An early writer, Justin (c.150 CE) describes a period of prayer and readings after which '… we salute one another with a kiss … Then bread and a cup of water and wine are brought to the president of the brethren. And he takes them and offers up praise and glory to the Father … through the name of the Son and of the Holy Spirit and gives thanks at length … all the people present say Amen, Amen. The food is called with us the Eucharist …'

Priests lie face-down during their ordination. This shows they are humble. They will soon be able to celebrate Mass in the Roman Catholic Church

> Then he poured some water into a basin and began to wash the disciples' feet.
>
> (John 13:5)

In this act of service Jesus reminded all Christian leaders that they were there to serve others. They were to minister to them and help them. This is why some Churches call their leaders the minister. In the Roman Catholic, Orthodox and Anglican Churches, the Eucharist (see unit 43) is carried out by a priest. In the Methodist and some other Churches it must be carried out by a fully ordained minister.

ORDINATION

Ordination is the ceremony in which a Church makes people deacons, priests or bishops (see unit 41). The ceremony usually includes the 'laying on of hands'. Some Christians think that this passes on spiritual power and authority. In many Churches, people think that the work of the priest or minister is so sacred that they need the authority of the Church to do it. Other Christian groups think this is not necessary. Priests or ministers must train for four years, or longer, before they can be ordained.

STRUCTURES

The Roman Catholic, Orthodox and Anglican Churches are led by bishops. The three levels of ministry are bishops, priests and deacons. Bishops are in charge of large areas called dioceses. Most priests work in a parish or local community. In Britain, deacons are people about to become priests.

An archbishop (senior bishop) may be in charge of the whole Church in a country. In the Orthodox Churches senior bishops are called patriarchs. This means 'great fathers'. In the Roman Catholic Church a group of senior ministers, called cardinals, is responsible for electing the Pope.

In England, the monarch is the Supreme Governor (Head) of the Church of England, and appoints bishops and archbishops. Many Protestant Churches elect moderators (national leaders) every year. They organize their groups through councils elected by individual Churches. Some denominations

KEY WORD

Ordination – the ceremony that makes a person a minister or priest

have both women and men as priests. These include the Lutheran Churches, the French Reformed Church, the Congregationalists, the Methodists and the Baptists. In 1994 the Church of England ordained its first women priests. Some members were not happy about this and have since joined the Roman Catholic Church. In the Roman Catholic and Eastern Orthodox Churches, only men can be priests.

WORK

As well as preaching and leading worship, ministers and priests do a wide range of work in the community. Their tasks include running youth groups, visiting prisoners, elderly people and those in hospital and comforting the bereaved, the sick, the lonely and the depressed.

FACTFILE

Peter, the rock of the Church

For many Christians, Peter was the first leader of the Church in Rome. Jesus said to him, 'I tell you Peter, you are a rock and on this rock foundation I will build my Church.'

ORDINATION

This ordination service in the Anglican Church is set out in the Alternative Service Book.

Before the Bishop ordains a priest, he reads out a list of the duties of a priest:

A priest is called by God to work with the bishop and his/her fellow-priests, as servant and shepherd among the people to whom he/she is sent. He/She is to proclaim the word of the Lord, to call his hearers to repentance, and in Christ's name to absolve, and to declare the forgiveness of sins. He/She is to baptize, and prepare the baptized for Confirmation. He/She is to preside at the celebration of the Holy Communion. He/She is to lead the people in prayer and worship, to intercede for them, to bless them in the name of the Lord, and to teach and encourage by word and example. He/She is to minister to the sick, prepare the dying for their death ... caring for the people ... and joining with them in a common witness to the world.

Almighty God, give us priests:
to establish the honour of your holy name;
to offer the holy sacrifice of the altar;
to give us Jesus in the holy sacrament;
to proclaim the faith of Jesus;
to baptize and to teach the young;
to tend your sheep;
to seek the lost;
to give pardon to the penitent sinner;
to bless our homes;
to pray for the afflicted;
to comfort the mourners;
to strengthen us in our last hour;
to commend our souls.

Almighty God, give us priests!
Holy father, you gave us Christ as the Shepherd of our souls; may your people always have priests who care for them with his great love.

... through Jesus Christ our Lord ... for ever and ever. Amen.

(Alternative Service Book)

INTRODUCTION

The major Christian festivals are based on the life of Jesus (see units 46–51 for more details). In this unit we look briefly at some of them. Some Churches celebrate more festivals than others. The Roman Catholic Church observes many festivals, including saints' days. Protestant Churches only observe the major festivals.

The two main sets of festivals are based around Christmas, which celebrates the birth of Jesus, and **Easter**, which remembers his death and resurrection. These festivals are observed by Christians all over the world.

In the Christian calendar, some festivals fall on the same day each year. Christmas Day is always 25 December. **Epiphany**, which is connected with Christmas, always falls on 6 January. Saints' days, which mark the lives of Christian saints, also fall on the same dates each year.

Other festival dates vary because they depend on the date of Easter. The date of Easter, which is always a Sunday, depends on the phases of the moon and can fall at any time between 21 March and 25 April.

In the Western Church, worship leaders wear robes of different colours for each season in the Church's year. They wear purple during times of fasting (e.g. during **Advent** and **Lent**). White is for the main festivals of Easter, Christmas, Ascension Day and some saints' days.

MAJOR CHRISTIAN FESTIVALS

Western

Epiphany: 6 January – Epiphany recalls the visit of the Wise Men who came from the East to see the new-born Christ. It is the last day of the Christmas period and it is when people put away their Christmas decorations until the following Christmas.

Ash Wednesday: February/March – This is the beginning of Lent. Lent lasts for 40 days. It recalls the time Jesus spent in the wilderness preparing for his ministry. In some Churches, there is a service on Ash Wednesday, when Christians have crosses drawn on their foreheads, with the ashes of the palm crosses from the previous year. This is to remind them of their mortality. Lent used to be a time of fasting. Some Christians give up a favourite food, such as chocolate, for 40 days.

Maundy Thursday: March/April – At a communion service on this day, people remember the Last Supper that Jesus spent with his disciples. In Britain the Queen gives out Maundy Money, traditionally to poor people, in memory of Jesus washing the feet of his disciples (see John 13:1–20).

Good Friday: March/April – Christians remember how Jesus died on the cross. It is called 'good' because Christians believe that Jesus died so that they can receive forgiveness for their sins. Traditionally, people eat hot cross buns, which are spiced buns decorated with a cross, on this day.

Easter Day: March/April – This feast day marks Jesus' resurrection, when he was seen alive by his followers. Some Christian parents hide Easter eggs, as symbols of new life, for their children to find.

Ascension Day: May/June – This day remembers Jesus' ascension into Heaven. In the Western Church, the Easter candle, lit during Easter, is snuffed on Ascension Day to mark Jesus' departure from the disciples.

Whit Sunday: May/June – This is another name for Pentecost, when God sent his Holy Spirit to the disciples and the Christian Church was founded. In some places, such as the north of England, there are public processions known as the Whit Walk. It is a popular time for baptisms (see unit 55).

Celebrating Easter in Guatamala, Central America

Advent Sunday: November/December – this is the beginning of the Church's calendar year.

Christmas Day: 25 December – The holy day that celebrates the birth of Jesus. No one knows when Christ was born, but by the mid-fourth century CE Christians were celebrating his birth at the winter solstice, which, according to astronomy, fell on 25 December.

Eastern

Orthodox festivals include:

Lenten Monday: February/March – The first day of fasting in preparation for Easter.

Easter Day/Pascha: March/April – Christians celebrate the Resurrection of Christ.

Pentecost: May/June – This word is from the Greek for 50 and is the same festival as the Western Christians' **Whitsun**.

FACTFILE

Harvest Festival

Harvest Thanksgiving does not appear in the list of official festivals of the Church. In Britain, many Christians give thanks to God for the fruits of the earth, usually on a Sunday in September or October, after the harvests have been gathered. It became popular following the first Harvest Festival held by the Reverend Robert Stephen Hawker in 1843, in the Cornish church of St Morwenna. Many tourists visit Morwenstowe to see the hut where Reverend Hawker used to compose poetry.

You can read the stories about the birth of Jesus in Matthew's Gospel, chapters 1 and 2, or Luke's Gospel, chapter 2.

ADVENT

Advent is the period of four weeks leading up to Christmas. During this time, Christians attend church services to read and think about the Bible stories and texts that they believe foretell the arrival of Jesus as God's special Saviour. Some Christian families have Advent calendars and Advent candles to celebrate that Christmas is coming.

CHRISTMAS

'Christmas' is the short form of 'Christ's Mass'. Nobody really knows the actual date of Jesus' birth. Early Christians did not think it was important. They were more concerned about who Jesus was and what he did.

The styles of worship at Christmas vary in the different Churches, but nearly all Christians go to church for this celebration. The focus of all the different rituals is the birth of Jesus, and the message that he is the Son of God.

For many Christians, the main celebration is the Eucharist (see unit 43). The service may include special music and a procession. The churches are decorated with flowers and evergreen branches. The first Eucharist of

Christmas starts at about 11.30 p.m. on Christmas Eve (the night before Christmas Day). This is called Midnight Mass and is a very popular service for Christians.

At Christmas, Christians thank God for giving his only Son to be born as a human being. This is called the Incarnation (see unit 7). At many Christmas services, the reading is from the first words of John's Gospel. These express the idea that Jesus is the 'Word of God' made flesh and that he is God. This is like saying that the birth of Jesus fulfils a promise made by God.

> Before the world was created, the Word already existed; he was with God and he was the same as God.
>
> (John 1:

Another reading may be from a prophecy revealed to the Prophet Isaiah 500 years previously.

> The people who walked in darkness have seen a great light. They lived in a land of shadows but now light is shining on them.
>
> (Isaiah 9:

FACTFILE

Stir-up Sunday

The Sunday before Advent is the last Sunday in the Church's calendar. It is traditionally called Stir-up Sunday. This is for two reasons. The first reason is that the prayer for the day begins 'Stir up, we beseech thee, O Lord, the wills of thy faithful people …'. The second reason is that this is the traditional time for making Christmas puddings and Christmas cakes. These rich mixtures need time to develop their full flavour.

… the child with his mother Mary … (Matthew 2:11)

REFLECTION

Forget the tinsel and the bright lights. Forget the carol singing and the loud parties. Forget the shops and trees laden with presents. All this is very enjoyable in the middle of winter, but doesn't have much to do with the meaning of the great Christian festival.

We forget that when 'Jesus was born in Bethlehem of Judea in the days of Herod the king', as the Gospel story tells us, it was not like that at all. The hotel where the Holy Family had hoped to shelter was full. So the baby Jesus, the 'Light of the World', first saw the light of day in an outhouse among the litter and the hay.

In a world where people were very poor and suffered injustice, a child was born. He was not born in some expensive private nursery. He was laid in a common manger, 'where oxen feed on hay'. For Christians all over the world, the birth of Jesus signifies the coming of God into the world. God took our human nature to show to us his Divine Nature. When He came, He found His first home to be a very make-shift affair.

The Christmas message is really about involvement. People with ideas who want to change things and influence others have to be involved. Christians believe that when Jesus was born God himself became involved in the life of human beings. He wanted to change things and make them better.

For centuries the Jewish people looked forward to a time when poverty, injustice, war, cruelty would give way to a reign of peace and righteousness. For Christians, this change is the event we enjoy when we celebrate Christmas. God himself was involved. He wanted to give the whole of His creation a better deal and a reason for living. Of course many Jewish people found it difficult to accept this. Today many people find it difficult to accept the stark reality of this event. They prefer to hide behind the sentimentality of the occasion.

God became involved. He took the form of a slave, a servant, meeting people as they were and where they were. How undignified! What a way to behave! Especially when seen by people so concerned about their status, their wealth, their power. People who always hide behind the 'right thing to do'.

When we ignore the needs of those who are suffering hunger or poverty, injustice or sickness, this is a sign that we reject God. Times don't seem to have changed for it was written down 2000 years ago that, 'he entered his own realm, and his own would not receive him' (John 1:1). Christ's birth tends to upset people's comfortable little lives, and they don't want this to happen. So, they try to keep him out in that outhouse where he was born. So they hide the true message in heaps of pretty tinsel and flashing neon lights.

But those who truly believe in him will try to follow his example. They know that he speaks to them of God in action. Then they will get involved, and will try to change the order of things and make the world a better place to live in.

(Adapted from an article by the Reverend Richard Roberts of the Church in Wales)

For Christians everywhere Easter is the most important festival. It celebrates the death and Resurrection of Jesus. Orthodox Christians often call it the 'Feast of Feasts'.

The preparation for Easter begins with the 40 days of Lent (not including Sundays) leading up to Easter. The celebrations continue for 50 days after Easter, until Whit-Sunday or Pentecost.

Lent represents the time Jesus spent alone in the wilderness.

THE TEMPTATION OF JESUS

Jesus returned from the Jordan full of the Holy Spirit and was led by the Spirit into the desert, where he was tempted by the Devil for forty days. In all that time he ate nothing, so that he was hungry when it was over.

The Devil said to him, 'If you are God's Son, order this stone to turn into bread.' But Jesus answered, 'The scripture says, "Man cannot live on bread alone."'

Then the Devil took him up and showed him in a second all the kingdoms of the world. 'I will give you all this power and all this wealth,' the Devil told him. '... A this will be yours, if you worship me.' Jesus answered, 'The scripture says, "Worship the Lord your God and serve only him!"'

Then the Devil took him to Jerusalem and set him on the highest point of the Temple, and said to him, 'If you are God's Son, throw yourself down from here. For the scripture says, "God will order his angels to take good care of you ... not even your feet will be hurt by the stones."' But Jesus answered, 'The scripture says, "Do not put the Lord you God to the test."'

(Luke 4:1–1

In the early Church, Christians did not eat any fish or meat products during Lent. Toda although some Christians fast strictly (do no eat) for part of the time, many others give u things like sweets or alcohol during Lent.

Christ in the wilderness

he meaning of Lent does not change. It is a me when Christians remember that Jesus ave up his life for the salvation of all human eings. First they remember his suffering, efore they have the joy of Easter when they emember his Resurrection from death.

HROVE TUESDAY

hrove Tuesday is the last day before Lent. lost people know this as Pancake Day. In he past, people used up all the good things, uch as butter and eggs, before they began he Lent fast. To be shriven is to be forgiven, o shrove means 'being forgiven'. This is the me when many Christians confess their sins nd ask God to forgive them. Some may go o a priest who gives them **absolution** orgiveness). Then they feel they can repare for Easter without the burden of sin.

SH WEDNESDAY

sh Wednesday is the first day of Lent. In hurch services on this day, the palm crosses small crosses made from palm leaves) that ere used in the previous year's Palm unday service, are burnt to ash. The ash is sed to make marks on people's foreheads n the shape of the cross.

UNDAYS IN LENT

ven in Lent, Sunday is a feast day. The ourth Sunday in Lent is known as Mothering unday. In the past, it was the Sunday when veryone tried to go to their 'Mother church' or a service. It is also a time when people how their gratitude to their mothers. The fth Sunday is Passion Sunday. Passion neans 'suffering' and this leads into the addest part of Lent. Ornaments and icons in he church may be covered up with purple loths. This gives a feeling of sorrow, sadness nd mourning. It is the last week before Holy Veek, which celebrates the last few days of esus' life.

POINTS OF VIEW

Origen (185–253 CE) was a teacher and priest in Alexandria and Caesarea. Son of a Christian martyr, Origen may also have been martyred. He wrote that people must not feel guilty about being tempted, but see that temptations can help them to understand themselves better.

The gifts which our soul has received are unknown to everyone except God. They are unknown even to ourselves. Through temptations they become known ... We know ourselves and can be aware of our wrongdoing. Temptations that come upon us serve the purpose of showing us who we really are and make clear the things that are in our heart.

FACTFILE

Fasting in the Church

One of the oldest Christian Churches is the Orthodox Church in Ethiopia which was founded in 325 CE. Fasting is taken very seriously in this Church. In short fasts, Christians may go without food altogether. In longer fasts they may have only a small, simple meal which is just enough to survive. The Ethiopian Church keeps the Great Lent fast, the Advent fast, the fast of the Apostles, the fast of Mary and the fast of Ninevah. They also fast on Wednesday and Friday every week.

Palm Sunday procession

Holy Week is often called 'The Passion'. It is the most solemn time in the Christian Year. Christians believe that at the end of this week, God's son was brutally killed on the cross by people who did not know any better.

SUNDAY – PALM SUNDAY

This Sunday celebrates Jesus' entry into Jerusalem, as described in the Gospels.

> The people who were in front and those who followed behind began to shout, 'Praise God! God bless him who comes in the name of the Lord!'
>
> (Mark 11:9)

The Gospels tell how people welcomed Jesus by laying palm leaves in his path as he rode into the city. On Palm Sunday some Christians gather outside the church, then walk in, in a procession. Some may walk in a procession round the church. Worshippers are given small crosses made from palm leaves. This is the last celebration before Christians remember the sad events of the rest of Holy Week.

THURSDAY – MAUNDY THURSDAY

Maundy comes from a Latin word *mandatum*, which means 'commandment'. The service on Maundy Thursday reminds Christians about Jesus' Last Supper with his disciples before his arrest and trial.

> While they were eating, Jesus took a piece of bread, gave a prayer of thanks, broke it, and gave it to his disciples. 'Take it,' he said, 'this is my body.' Then he took a cup, gave thanks to God, and handed it to them; and they all drank from it. Jesus said, 'This is my blood which is poured out for many, which seals God's covenant.'
>
> (Mark 14:22–

This meal has become an important sacrament – the Eucharist. John's Gospel describes how Jesus gave his disciples a new commandment at the Last Supper:

> … love one another. As I have loved you so you must love one another … then everyone will know that you are my disciples.
>
> (John 13:3

RIDAY – GOOD FRIDAY

fter the Last Supper, Jesus was arrested and
ied. On the Friday he was crucified by the
omans. This Friday is called 'good' because
hristians believe that Jesus' death was the
reatest act of goodness. He gave his life for
e sake of humankind.

They took Jesus to a place called
Golgotha, which means 'The Place of the
Skull'. There they tried to give him wine
mixed with a drug called myrrh, but
Jesus would not drink it. Then they
crucified him … It was nine o'clock in
the morning when they crucified him.
The notice of the accusation against him
said: 'The King of the Jews'. They also
crucified two bandits with Jesus, one on
his right and the other on his left.

(Mark 15:22–8)

In many Churches, services on Good Friday
last from noon until three in the afternoon.
The churches are dark and sombre, like the
mood of the Christians inside the church.
They feel very sad because they believe that
the death of Jesus was the time when human
beings denied God.

POINTS OF VIEW

- Would you know your Lord's
  meaning in this thing? Learn it
  well: love was his meaning.
  (Julian of Norwich, *c.*1342–1420)

- Nails would not have held the
  God-man fast to the cross had not
  love held him there.
  (Catherine of Siena, 1347–80)

FACTFILE

Maundy Thursday
On Maundy Thursday, after the
evening Eucharist, the altar is stripped
of all the rich cloths, silver candlesticks
and ornaments. This is done during
readings from the Prayer Book.
Suddenly, when the priest reads the
words '… and they all fled', the
church is plunged into darkness and
everyone leaves in silence.

'The Crucifixion' by Salvador Dali

49 THE RESURRECTION

SUNDAY – EASTER SUNDAY

The Gospels say that on the third day after his death on the cross, Jesus 'rose from the dead'. This is known as the Resurrection.

> After the Sabbath was over, Mary Magdalene, Mary the mother of James, and Salome bought spices to go and anoint the body of Jesus. … On the way they said to one another, 'Who will roll away the stone for us from the entrance to the tomb?' … Then they looked up and saw that the stone had already been rolled back. So they entered the tomb, where they saw a young man sitting on the right, wearing a white robe, and they were alarmed. 'Don't be alarmed,' he said. 'I know you are looking for Jesus of Nazareth, who was crucified. He is not here – he has been raised!'
>
> (Mark 16:1–6)

For Christians, the Resurrection of Jesus is the most important event described in the New Testament. It is a wonderful and miraculous act of God. St Paul explains the meaning of the Resurrection like this:

> But the truth is that Christ has been raised from death, as the guarantee that those who sleep in death will also be raised. For just as death came by means of a man, in the same way the rising from death comes by means of a man. For just as all people die because of their union with Adam, in the same way all will be raised to life because of their union with Christ.
>
> (I Corinthians 15:20–22)

THE RESURRECTION IN THE NEW TESTAMENT

All the books of the New Testament mention belief in the Resurrection. The Resurrection is

The Resurrection is at the heart of Christianity

at the heart of Christianity. According to the Gospels, when Jesus was crucified the disciples ran away, terrified and in despair. Yet something happened that gave them the courage to meet together again and to go out into a harsh world to preach his message.

The Epistles in the New Testament do not describe the Resurrection, but refer to the victory of Jesus over death, and the inner feelings of new life that Christians experience

> If the spirit of God, who raised Jesus from death, lives in you, then he who raised Christ from death will also give life to your mortal bodies …
>
> (Romans 8:11

The four Gospel writers describe the Resurrection as a huge triumph, with its message of hope. Despite the fact that Jesus died and his life may have seemed a failure, the Resurrection shows God's blessing on Jesus. It confirms God's promise that he would save humankind, and that darkness and death will be turned to light and life.

WORSHIP

In many churches people stay awake all night on the Saturday, waiting for the dawn of Easter Sunday. Inside the churches, the mood of gloom and sadness changes to become bright and joyful. Ornaments of silver and gold are put back in their places, every possible area of the church is decorated with bright colours and spring flowers. Large Easter candles, called Paschal candles, are lit and carried in. Church bells ring and everyone joins in the celebration, singing joyful hymns. This is the most important Sunday in the Christian year. For Christians it celebrates the turning point of history.

FACTFILE

Community of the Resurrection

In Mirfield, West Yorkshire, there is an Anglican community called The Community of the Resurrection. It was first set up in Oxford in 1892 by Charles Gore but moved to Mirfield in 1898. The community trains ordinands, who are people training to be priests. It also is involved in pastoral and educational work in South Africa and Zimbabwe. A famous ex-student is Trevor Huddlestone, who did a lot to stop apartheid in South Africa.

POINTS OF VIEW

- If Christ was to raise a new life like his own in every man, then every man must have had in the inmost spirit of his life, a seed of Christ, or Christ as a seed of heaven …

  (William Law)

- Jesus dares to confuse the space known as earth. The resurrection is nothing if not a conquest of time and place (death on Golgotha) by space – that is by an empty (space-filled) tomb where sadness and death are no longer granted place. Where grief comes to an end.

  (Matthew Fox)

ACCORDING TO LUKE...

On the day that the women found the empty tomb, two of Jesus' followers were going to a village near Jerusalem. They were talking about all the things that had happened. As they talked, Jesus himself drew near and walked along with them. They saw him but somehow did not recognize him.

They told Jesus all about the crucifixion, and it was only as he sat down to eat with them, and broke the bread for the meal, that they recognized him. But then he disappeared. They rushed back to Jerusalem to tell the disciples, but found them already highly excited and saying, 'The Lord is risen indeed!'

(from Luke 24:13–35)

We have seen that Easter is the most important festival in the Christian year. The Reflections are taken from interviews with three Christians from different traditions. Each tries to explain what they feel about their own Easter experiences. The first is from Tim Richards, a Protestant from Wales. The second comes from Mario Constantinou, a young member of the Greek Orthodox Church. The third is from Caitlin McKenny, a Catholic living in Belfast.

REFLECTION 1

I try to go into a church every morning during Easter week, to sit quietly, think, and sometimes pray. Easter is a mystery. Almost 2000 years ago, in a remote corner of the Roman Empire there was a new teaching. Jesus' preaching lasted only three years and ended in defeat. The preacher was executed. But on the eve of his death, he prophesied that the Good News he had brought would be preached 'unto all nations'. Today the Gospel has been translated into more than 600 languages.

This is a miracle. It is part of the miracle that began when Mary Magdalene found that the stone of the tomb had been rolled away. Jesus Christ rose from the grave. The Gospel writers tell us that Jesus rose physically from the dead. Tertullian (c.160–230 CE) wrote that what is raised is flesh and blood. I believe that a Supreme Power who can create the universe can do anything – most of all raise up a Messenger from the blood-stained hill of Calvary.

(Tim Richards)

REFLECTION 2

Lent, when people share in the fast, is a time for reflection and learning about oneself and Christ. Every day with thousands of others we descend upon the small churches in Athens and offer our prayers to God. Then on Holy Friday, the day when Christ gave us his ultimate sacrifice, the bells toll throughout our land. The body of our Saviour lies covered in flowers in all the village churches. In the churches the great liturgy takes place. Twelve passages are read from the Bible, while we hold lighted candles. The winding sheet, a cloth symbolizing the broken body of our Saviour, is placed in the middle of the church, like a coffin at a funeral.

On the Saturday, we symbolize Christ's burial by carrying the winding sheet around the church three times. Later the priests change their vestments from the colours of despair to the whiteness of joy and life. At midnight the bells throughout the world chime. The priests wait outside the closed church door – a symbol of the tomb. The doors are opened and the priests come in with candles and lights. The church is a sea of light as we embrace each other, 'Christ is risen' echoes through the church, 'He is risen indeed!'

(Mario Constantinou)

REFLECTION 3

On Holy Thursday we celebrate Mass. The priest will wash the feet of some of the congregation. He acts out Christ's humility. Afterwards all ornaments are removed from the altar. On the Friday we have a three-hour service of readings and hymns.

The Saturday is a day of vigil (waiting). All Christian worship springs from this night. Through drama and poetry we act out the central events of our faith. Here we hope and trust that a world of justice and unity will be born from our suffering world. A large candle marked with alpha and omega, the first and last letters of the Greek alphabet, is carried into the darkened church. Its light drives out the darkness. Then the people sing: 'Rejoice: Christ has conquered'. A service of readings follows, when the whole of history is recalled, from the alpha of Creation to the omega of the Resurrection. This is a time of great joy and hope. The bells ring; we sing 'Glory to God in the highest'. Mass is celebrated. Tonight and again tomorrow the great mystery of Mass floods my soul with a peace that goes beyond any normal understanding. The holiness of this shared holy meal is the highest form of human activity. The risen Lord, the risen Christ is with us in the bread we break and the wine we drink.

(Caitlin McKenny)

FACTFILE

New Fire

This is how the ceremony of the 'New Fire' is celebrated:

Before sunrise on Easter Sunday morning, the priest and members of the congregation meet outside the church. If it is a country church there may be a bonfire already set up. If it is the town it may be a small fire on a barbecue. A spark is struck from a flint and this sets light to the fire. A burning branch is taken into church. It is used to light the Paschal Candle. If the timing is right, the sun rises at about this time and shines through the east window. At a signal from the priest, the congregation will sing out 'Alleluia! Christ is risen! He is risen indeed! Alleluia!'

An Easter procession in Brazil

A procession in South India, celebrating the Ascension

ASCENSION DAY

Jesus is taken up to heaven

On the Thursday that is 40 days after Easter Sunday, Christians remember Jesus' ascension – when he was taken up into heaven. This was the last day that the disciples saw him on earth. In churches, Christians remember the ascension with special prayers and readings from the Bible. The Bible describes it like this.

> When the apostles met together with Jesus, they asked him, 'Lord, will you at this time give the Kingdom back to Israel?' Jesus said to them, 'The times and occasions are set by my Father's own authority, and it is not for you to know when they will be. But when the Holy Spirit comes upon you, you will be filled with power, and you will be witnesses for me in Jerusalem, in all Judea and Samaria and to the ends of the earth.' After saying this, he was taken up to heaven as they watched him, and a cloud hid him from their sight.

(Acts 1:6–9)

WHITSUN

It says in the Acts of the Apostles that seven weeks after the Resurrection, on the day of the Jewish festival of Pentecost, the disciples received power from the Holy Spirit (see Acts 2:1–4 and unit 20). Christians believe that the Spirit was given to the disciples and to the whole of humankind on this day.

Many Christians think of Pentecost (or Whitsun) as the birthday of the Christian Church. It is a tradition for new members to be baptized on this day. People dress in white. This symbolizes purity. It is the reason why the day became known as White Sunday, or Whitsun.

TRINITY SUNDAY

Trinity Sunday is the Sunday after Whitsun. On Trinity Sunday, many Christians remember that although they believe in only one God, they think of God in three ways: God the Father, God the Son and God the Holy Spirit.

In some Christian groups, people who have completed their training for the ministry are ordained on Trinity Sunday. This is the last major festival in the Church's calendar, before Advent.

THE TRINITY

The idea of the Trinity is very difficult to explain. However, Christians believe it is important to try to understand it, because it is central to their beliefs about God. The Trinity was described in unit 8, but it is useful to think about some of the main ideas again.

The Trinity is not described in the Bible, but there are hints about the three-way nature of God in Matthew 28:19 and 2 Corinthians 13:14. As the early Church tried to explain the meaning of Christ's life and teaching, the idea of the Trinity grew. At the Councils of Nicaea and Constantinople the Bishops agreed that both Jesus Christ, as Son of God, and the Holy Spirit are the same being as God the Father. They are fully God, without dividing God. The idea of the Trinity is used to describe the whole nature of God, as shown through Christ's life on earth. It can be put like this:

God was present in the Son (Jesus). Humans can know God through knowing Jesus. He is also known as the Father, who 'sends' the Son. He is also the Holy Spirit, who works in the hearts and minds of men and women. But it is the same God in each case. The words 'Father, Son and Holy Spirit' refer to one and the same God.

QUOTE

If Christian faith speaks of a real revelation of God, then 'Father, Son and Holy Spirit' don't refer just to the way human beings see God. They refer to God himself … He is Himself, Father, Son and Spirit, one God.

(Claude Welch – *The Doctrine of the Trinity in Contemporary Theology*)

FACTFILE

Life-changing Spirit

According to St Luke, the author of Acts, the Holy Spirit changed the lives of the disciples. It also changed the lives of people round them:

There were Jews living in Jerusalem, religious men who had come from every country in the world. When they heard this noise, a large crowd gathered. They were all excited, because each one of them heard the believers speaking in his own language. In amazement and wonder they exclaimed, 'These people who are talking like this are Galileans! How is it, then, that all of us hear them speaking in our own native languages? We are from … Mesopotamia, Judaea and Cappadocia; from Pontus and Asia … from Egypt and … Libya … Some of us are from Rome … from Crete and Arabia – yet all of us hear them speaking in our own languages …!' Amazed and confused, they kept asking each other, 'What does this mean?'

(Acts 2:5–12)

Christians believe that they can come closer to God through prayer

Christians believe that they can communicate with God through prayer. Most Christians pray on their own as well as in groups. God can be their own personal God, as well as the God of the whole world.

TYPES OF PRAYER

Here are some of the types of prayer that Christians use.

- **Adoration** – praising God for his greatness, power, wisdom and love.

- **Confession** – realizing their own weakness, the Christian may ask God for forgiveness.

- **Intercession** – praying on behalf of someone else. The person thinks about the needs of others and asks God to help people who are sick, poor, lonely.

- **Petition** – asking God for personal help.

- **Thanksgiving** – thanking God for his goodness and praising him for his love.

MEDIATORS

When Christians pray to God, many of them end with the words 'through Jesus Christ our Lord'. This is because many Christians think that God is too great to approach directly and they need to ask Jesus for help. The Bible refers to Jesus as an advocate and an intercessor. Both words mean 'mediator', or someone who speaks on behalf of someone else. Protestants believe that only Jesus can mediate between themselves and God. Others, including Roman Catholics, may ask saints, such as Mary the Mother of Jesus, to act as mediator.

Christians do not all pray in the same way or at set times. Some use their own words. Others prefer to use set forms of prayer. Christians also use another form of prayer called contemplation (see unit 36).

FACTFILE

When you pray...
Closing their eyes while praying helps a person to keep their thoughts on God alone. Placing the hands together, like the girl in the photograph, is an old way of asking for a special favour.

POINTS OF VIEW

The great psychologist, Jung, has written that there are two ways to lose your soul. One of these is to worship a God outside you … A lot of church-goers in the West have been losing their souls for generations … They have attended religious events where prayer is addressed to a god outside.

(Matthew Fox)

THREE PRAYERS

Look at these three prayers. What types of prayer do you think they are?

Lord make me an instrument of
  thy peace,
where there is hatred, let me
  sow love;
where there is injury, pardon;
where there is discord, union;
where there is doubt, faith;
where there is despair, hope;
where there is darkness, light;
where there is sadness, joy;
for your mercy and for your
  truth's sake.
Amen.

(Prayer of St Francis)

And in the name of every creature
under heaven we too praise your
glory as we say, 'Holy, holy, holy
Lord, God of power and might,
heaven and earth are full of
  your glory.
Hosanna in the highest.'

(Roman Catholic Sunday Missal)

Christ has no body now on earth but
  yours;
yours are the only hands with which
  he can do his work,
yours are the only feet with which he
  can go about the world,
yours are the only eyes through
  which his compassion can shine
  forth upon a troubled world.

(Teresa of Avila)

QUOTES

- Why, O Lord, is it so hard for me to keep my heart directed toward you? Why do the many little things I want to do, and the many people I know, keep crowding into my mind, even during the hours that I am totally free to be with you and you alone? Why does my mind wander off in so many directions, and why does my heart desire the things that lead me astray? Are you not enough for me? …

Please accept my distractions, my fatigue, my irritations, and my faithless wanderings … You love me with a greater love than I can love myself. You offer me more than I can desire. Look at me, see me in all my misery and inner confusion, and let me sense your presence in the midst of my turmoil.

(Henri Nouwen – Trappist monk)

- Instead of supposing that one great God is thinking about the answer to millions of different problems of all the individuals in the world, is it not more reasonable to suppose that some action is set in motion by prayer … this uplifting power somehow activates the … solution-providing mechanism which would otherwise not be possible.

(Sir Alistair Hardy)

Many Christians use the Bible, a **rosary**, a crucifix and icons to help them in their prayers.

THE BIBLE

REFLECTION

In order to hear God in the silence it is useful to fix your mind on some image which will help inspire meditation. There is no better source for such inspiration than the Bible … We learn from the Bible how to offer our prayers and the guidelines we should follow.

(Reverend P. B. Martin)

THE ROSARY

Many Roman Catholics use a rosary when they pray. A rosary is made up of five sets of ten beads. Each set of beads is called a decade (A). Each decade is separated by a bead which is more spaced out than the others (B). As they count the beads while they pray, Roman Catholics are able to contemplate (think about) some of the main events in the lives of Jesus and Mary. At each bead the person praying repeats the *Ave Maria* – the Hail Mary (see unit 12).

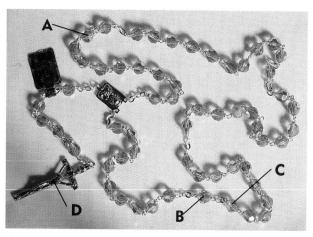

At the first bead of the decade (C) the person praying says the **Pater Noster** ('Our Father …', see opposite). At the last bead of the decade, the person says the *Gloria Patri*:

Glory be to the Father and to the Son and to the Holy Spirit. As it was in the beginning, is now and ever shall be, world without end. Amen.

THE CRUCIFIX

The crucifix (D) is a cross with an image of Jesus on it. It hangs from the string of beads attached by five more beads. These beads stand for a *Pater Noster*, three *Ave Marias* and a *Gloria*. When the person comes to the crucifix they say the Apostles' Creed (see unit 5). As well as forming part of a rosary, crucifixes are often worn as necklaces, on a chain. Larger crucifixes are made as statues.

ICONS

Icons are important for Orthodox Christian prayer. Icons are religious paintings of Jesus, Mary (see opposite), saints and angels. They are richly decorated. They are not just portraits of good people; they are meant to express their inner characters. It is the meaning of the picture that is important. Orthodox Christians treat icons with great **reverence**. They do not pray to the icons. They use the icons to help them focus their prayers on God.

THE LORD'S PRAYER

In Matthew 6:9–13, Jesus told his disciples, 'This is how you should pray', and gave them a prayer that is now known as the Lord's Prayer. All Christian groups use the Lord's Prayer. It is the most important prayer in Christianity. It is a model for prayers of adoration, confession and petition.

Our Father in heaven,
May your holy name be honoured;
may your Kingdom come;
may your will be done on earth as it is in
heaven.
Give us today the food we need.
Forgive us the wrongs we have done,
as we forgive the wrongs that others
have done to us.
Do not bring us to hard testing, but keep
us safe from the Evil One.

(Matthew 6:9–13, *Good News Bible*)

HE JESUS PRAYER

he Jesus Prayer – 'O Lord Jesus Christ, Son
f God, have mercy on me' – is especially
mportant to Orthodox Christians. Orthodox
mystics used to repeat this prayer
continuously. Some believed that the name
of Jesus was itself divine, so repeating it
continuously would bring direct
communication with God. This prayer could
be used in meditation, with a particular
posture (head bowed, chin on chest, eyes
fixed on the position of the heart) and
controlled breathing. This helped them to
concentrate.

THE PRACTICE OF THE PRESENCE OF GOD

Brother Lawrence (1605–91) was a French
soldier who became a monk. He lived in
constant prayer. He called this 'the practice
of the presence of God'. At the beginning of
the day be prayed to be in the presence of
God as he worked. He said, 'the time of
business does not with me differ from the
time of prayer'.

con of the Black Madonna of Czestochowa

KEY WORDS

Doxology – a set of words, used at the
end of a prayer, praising God, e.g.

'For thine is the kingdom, the power
and the glory, for ever and ever, Amen.'

Amen – 'Let it be'

FACTFILE

Humble before God

Christians may pray seated or standing
up, kneeling or prostrate (face down)
on the ground. People usually bow
their heads when in prayer. All this is
to show that human beings are
humble before God. Some people
make the sign of the cross as they
pray. Others are quite still.

INTRODUCTION

A pilgrimage is a journey made for a religious reason. People who go on pilgrimage are called pilgrims.

Pilgrims are not just tourists on holiday. They travel to places that they believe are holy or sacred. Every year, pilgrims from many different religions make these special religious journeys. Anyone can be a pilgrim: rich or poor, male or female, old or young.

Pilgrims try to reach a holy place where they can feel close to their god and their religion. Some holy places may be in great cities, but some are high in the mountains. Pilgrims may walk great distances.

PILGRIMAGE AS SELF-UNDERSTANDING

Pilgrimage is not only a journey to a place, it can also refer to the human journey through life, from birth to death. In this way, it is our inner journey: as we grow, we begin to understand more about ourselves. According to an old saying, 'Know yourself and you will know the universe'. This means that getting to know yourself helps you to understand what is going on outside and around you.

PILGRIM'S PROGRESS

John Bunyan (1628–88) wrote *Pilgrim's Progress* while he was in prison for preaching the Gospel without proper permission. It became a best-seller. The story describes the journey of a man named Christian and his friend, Hopeful, from the City of Destruction to the Celestial City. On the way he meets many obstacles and difficulties. The story symbolizes the Christian life.

PLACES OF PILGRIMAGE

In the Middle Ages, pilgrimage was a very important part of life for many Christians. There are many Christian holy places all over

Pilgrims crowd the streets of Santiago de Compostela

the world. In this unit we shall look at a few of them. For devout pilgrims they are all places where God's power has been shown in action. When they visit these holy sites, pilgrims believe they can share in God's grace.

Millions of pilgrims from all over the world go to Spain to visit the shrine of St James at Santiago de Compostela. Santiago is the Spanish name for St James. The pilgrims go to pay respect to the disciple who may have visited Spain to preach the Gospel. According to tradition, after Herod Agrippa killed St James, his body was brought from Jerusalem to Spain. Some pilgrims even walk across the mountains to reach his tomb. This is called the 'way of St James'. Many of the pilgrims wear cockle-shell badges because the site is near the sea and this is the emblem of pilgrims to Santiago.

Rome in Italy is important because of the part it played in the development of the early Church. Deep underground are the Catacombs where early Christians secretly met and worshipped to avoid persecution. The Vatican is also in Rome. It is the centre of the Roman Catholic Church and is where the Pope lives.

Lourdes is in the Pyrenean Mountains in Southern France. It attracts huge crowds of pilgrims every year. There is a small grotto,

ith a spring of water. In 1858, when she
as fourteen years old, Bernardette
ubirous claimed to have seen eighteen
sions of the Virgin Mary. The spring of
ater appeared when she had these visions
nd people claimed to have been healed as
 result of bathing in the water. An official
ilgrimage took place in 1862. Now
hristians from all over the world come to
orship and pray for healing from diseases.
 1958, the centenary year, six million
ilgrims visited Lourdes. Bernadette was
anonized in 1933 (see unit 10).

Other shrines have become places of
ilgrimage, usually because someone has
ad a vision, and this was followed by a
iracle. Some examples are Grenoble in
rance, Ilare in Croatia, Knock in Ireland and
atima in Portugal.

 Britain, Canterbury became a popular
entre of pilgrimage in the Middle Ages. The
hrine of St Thomas à Becket (1118–70) is
ere. St Thomas was murdered in the
athedral by four knights of Henry II after
ecket had disagreed with the King. Now
anterbury is the centre of power of the
hurch of England.

Valsingham in Norfolk is another place of
ilgrimage that became popular in the
Aiddle Ages. People believed that the Holy
House of Nazareth, where Jesus had been
rought up, had miraculously been
ransported to this small town in Norfolk. The
hrine was destroyed during the Reformation,
ut was restored in 1897. The priory is
isited by Roman Catholic and Protestant
Christians. It is dedicated to Our Lady
f Walsingham.

Many Christians try to visit the Holy Land:
srael. They visit the places where Jesus lived
nd travelled. In Jerusalem they can walk
long the Via Dolorosa (the Way of the
Cross) where Jesus carried his cross. They
an visit the Church of the Holy Sepulchre,

said to be built over the place where he died.
They may also visit the Garden of
Gethsemane, Bethlehem, Nazareth, Galilee
and Capernaum.

Mount Athos, in Greece, is the centre of
Orthodox monasticism and welcomes many
pilgrims every year.

QUOTE

Ninian Smart, a modern theologian,
says that God has marked out certain
places to become holy. These are the
places that pilgrims travel to visit. He
said, 'The earthly voyage is an echo of
life, which is in itself a pilgrimage.'

FACTFILE

St Helen, 255–330 CE
A famous early Christian, St Helen is
sometimes called the 'Mother of
Pilgrims'. She was the mother of the
Emperor Constantine and was an
enthusiastic Christian. She visited the
Holy Land where she founded
churches on the Mount of Olives and
at Bethlehem. After a visit to Rome
she wrote to her religious adviser
because she had seen different ways
of worshipping. She received the reply,
'When in Rome, do as the Romans
do!' This has now become a well-
known saying.

All Christian groups except the Salvation Army and the Society of Friends practise baptism. This is how new members enter the Church. In many churches, the font is near the door of the church to symbolize this entry. In Baptist churches, the baptistery is nearer the centre of the building.

Baptism is very symbolic for Christians. Baptism is a symbol of:

- renunciation (giving up) of sin – the person being baptized, or the parents of the infant, must promise to repent and give up their sins

- renewal – it is the beginning of a new life with God

- cleansing – the water used in baptism is c symbol for spiritual and inner cleanliness.

REFLECTION

Most religions regard water as a powerful symbol. The early Church adopted the practice of baptizing converts in obedience to the instructions Jesus had given to his disciples (Matthew 28:19–20). It was through studying the importance of baptism to the early Church that Baptists laid so much stress on the practice which has given them their name.

Most Baptist churches nowadays have a baptistry built into the floor of the church. It's a great day when the pool comes into use. The candidate approaches the minister some weeks before and requests baptism. The minister questions the candidate to make sure he/she has made a personal commitment to Jesus Christ and understands a little of what it means to follow him. Then comes the long-awaited day. If the candidate is a girl, she will be dressed in a special white baptismal gown. If a boy, he will come dressed in shirt and flannels.

… In many churches the candidate is expected to stand by the pool and to give a statement about how he or she came to faith in Christ. Then once the candidate has entered the water, the minister pronounces his or her name and plunges the candidate beneath the waters, baptizing him or her 'in the name of the Father, the Son and the Holy Spirit'…

What does baptism mean? Baptism, like art or drama, needs to be experienced rather than explained. The New Testament teaches that baptism is a kind of death and resurrection. It marks the end of an old quality of life and the commencement of a totally new quality of life, lived out in the company of all other Christians. Looking at the New Testament, baptism is a kind of 'statement' – the ceremony speaks very clearly of the way Jesus died and rose again, and how a person needs to be made clean; it is also an act of 'commitment' – just as the candidate has taken off his normal clothing and put on his special baptismal attire, so in life he has put the past behind him, and put on a totally new kind of life altogether. Baptism is also a 'gift', it is the place where one may receive forgiveness of sins and a means of receiving God's Holy Spirit into life. It is also the gateway into membership of Christ's Church.

(John Wood)

KEY IDEA

Baptism is an outward, visible sign of rebirth. It marks the start of a new life. The water symbolizes the sin being washed from the life of the person being baptized.

believer's baptism

INFANT BAPTISM

Most Christian groups baptize infants, but Baptists and some others believe that an infant is too young to understand what is going on. They feel also that children should not be baptized unless their parents intend to bring them up in the Christian Church.

CONFIRMATION

When infant baptism became common, Christians saw the need for a service in which young Christians could confirm the baptismal promises that had been made for them. This service became known as confirmation. The person being confirmed should be old enough to understand the promises they are making. A bishop usually conducts confirmation services.

Candidates for confirmation have to answer set questions as a group, such as:

- 'Do you turn to Christ?'
- 'Do you repent of your sins?'
- 'Do you renounce evil?'

The bishop asks, 'Do you believe and trust in God the Father, who made the world?' Then the candidates kneel in front of the bishop who places his hands upon the head of each one in turn. In the Roman Catholic and some Anglican Churches the bishop puts some oil on their foreheads. The oil symbolizes the gifts of the Holy Spirit.

In Orthodox Churches, the oil, or chrism, is applied straight after baptism at a ceremony of chrismation.

Methodists and United Reformed Churches do not have confirmation services. Instead, people become 'full members' when they publicly confess their faith.

FACTFILE

Christening robes

In some churches a white christening robe is placed on the child being baptized, with these words, 'We place this white vesture upon this child, as a token of the innocence bestowed upon him/her by God's grace in this holy Sacrament of Baptism.' Then the minister may hand a lighted candle to one of the godparents, saying, 'We give this lighted candle to this child as a sign of the light of Christ and of the grace of Baptism.'

'I take thee…'

MARRIAGE

I take thee to be my wedded husband
  (or wife)
to have and to hold
from this day forward
for better for worse
for richer for poorer
in sickness and in health
to love and to cherish
'til death us do part
according to God's holy law
and thereto I give thee my troth (promise).

(*The Book of Common Prayer*)

For Christians, the joining of a woman and a man in holy matrimony symbolizes the union of Christ with his Church. They believe that in their love for each other, married couples can learn about God's love. Jesus taught that God's purpose was that marriage should last for life:

In the beginning … God made them male and female … and for this reason a man will leave his father and mother and unite with his wife, and the two will become one.

(Mark 10:6–8)

Christians believe that marriage is the proper relationship for people to have sexual intercourse, to have children and to give mutual support. All denominations teach that marriage is intended to be a life-long commitment.

The Baptist Union of Great Britain

The couple vow to God that they will remain married for life. It is a very serious promise. Baptists believe that the words of the marriage ceremony are spoken by the couple, but the marriage is made by God. God unites the two people.

The Church of England

Priests conduct the marriage ceremony in the Church of England. They believe the ceremony celebrates God's gift of marriage.

The Methodist Church

Methodists believe marriage is for life. They believe that partners in a marriage should give each other companionship and support each other as equals. Marriage is also for procreation (having babies) and bringing up children. It is God's will for most men and women to marry.

The Roman Catholic Church

Roman Catholics see marriage as a **vocation** and a sacrament. Here are some extracts from a Roman Catholic marriage service:

Father, you have made the union of man and wife so holy a mystery that it symbolizes the marriage of Christ and his Church.

Look with love upon this woman, your daughter, now joined to her husband by marriage … Give her the grace of peace and love … May her husband put his trust in her and recognize that she is his equal and the heir with him to the life of grace. May he always honour her and love her…Keep them faithful in marriage… through Jesus Christ our Lord. Amen.

DIVORCE

Sometimes marriages do not work and couples decide to separate. Since the 1969 Divorce Act it is easier to obtain a divorce in Britain. Generally, Christians believe that every effort should be made to keep couples together.

> Christian teaching is that marriage is the life-long union of the partners and is therefore in principle indissoluble [cannot be broken]. However, with other Christians … the Methodist Church recognizes that for a variety of reasons marriages do die … separation or divorce may be unavoidable.
>
> (Methodist Conference statement)

The Roman Catholic view

The Roman Catholic Church teaches that divorce is a civil matter. Couples cannot be divorced in the sight of the Church. The Church will not bless a second marriage if a partner of the first marriage is still alive.

However, the Church can grant an **annulment**. This means the marriage is null and void, as if it never happened. It can do this if there was some reason why the marriage was not valid, e.g. if there was:

- lack of consent (somebody was forced into a marriage)

- lack of judgement (somebody didn't understand what marriage is really about)

- inability to carry out the duties of marriage (perhaps somebody is mentally ill)

- lack of intention (one partner intends not to have children)

The Church allows **dissolution** of a marriage in some serious cases, for example if one member was not baptized, or for a reason such as impotence. Dissolution means the marriage bonds are broken.

FACTFILE

Can the couple marry?

Before the marriage ceremony begins, the minister says to the congregation:

We have come together in the presence of God to witness the marriage of this man and this woman, and to pray for them. Marriage is a gift from God to his people. Holy Scripture compares it with the union of Christ with his Church. It should therefore be held in honour by all people. It must not be entered upon lightly or thoughtlessly, but responsibly and reverently. God calls men and women to the married state so that their love may be made holy in life-long union; that they may bring up their children to grow in grace and learn to love him; and that they may honour, help and comfort one another both in prosperity [when things go well] and adversity [when there is hardship].

If any of you is aware of any just impediment [legal objection] to this marriage, you are to declare it now.

(*The Service Book of the Church in Wales*)

The minister then asks the couple if they know any reason why they ought not to be married, according to the law of the land, or the law of the Church.

INTRODUCTION

In this unit we look in more detail at the Roman Catholic and Anglican views on marriage, the family, divorce and contraception.

ATTITUDES TO MARRIAGE

In the sixteenth century, after the Reformation (see unit 21) the Roman Catholic and Protestant Churches separated. They developed different ideas about moral issues. More recently, the Roman Catholic and Anglican Churches have talked together. They have found that they still have similar beliefs about the Christian life and agree about many aspects of their faith. Here are two areas where there is total agreement:

Human sexuality

- In the Bible human sexuality is part of God's creation (Genesis 1:27–8 and 2:24; The Song of Songs; Ephesians 5:21–32).

- Sexual energy can create and it can destroy. It needs to be part of an ordered life.

- Sexual self-centredness is a sin that leads to personal and social destruction.

- Sexual energy must be controlled. It must be directed towards marriage or celibacy. Only in this way can humans find true happiness and fulfilment.

- Sexual relationships relate to society as well as to individuals. This affects other issues such as justice, the exploitation of women and the protection of children.

Marriage and the family

- Marriage and family life are gifts from God for human well-being and happiness.

- Within marriage and family life, the physical expression of sexuality can find its true fulfilment.

- In procreation (having babies) and rearing children, the couple share with God in bringing new life into being (Genesis 1:27–9).

- Marriage is not a human invention, it is God-given.

- Marriage requires commitment, reciprocal (two-way) love, trust and mutual support.

- Marriage is a vocation.

- The promise to love one another, made between husband and wife, is like the love of God for his people (Hosea 2:19–21). Marriage is a sign of God's faithful love and a part of it, so there is something sacramental (see unit 41) about it.

DIVORCE

In real life, marriages do not always reflect this life-long promise of love. The Roman Catholic and Anglican Churches differ in their views about separation, divorce and remarriage.

The Anglican Church

In 1857, laws about marriage in England were transferred from the jurisdiction (authority) of the Church to the State, and became a civil matter. Divorce because of adultery became legal. However, the Church of England refused to allow remarriage in

The irretrievable breakdown of marriage

church. This is still hotly debated within the Anglican Church and different provinces (areas) have different rules. Some allow remarriage in Church, while others will bless a couple after a civil ceremony.

The Roman Catholic Church

The Council of Trent declared that marriages could not be dissolved. Sacramental marriages (where both partners are baptized members) cannot be dissolved. The Church has different rules for couples where one or both partners are not baptized. These are called natural marriages.

Both kinds of marriage are indissoluble if they have been consummated (sexual intercourse has taken place). However, the Church will sometimes allow natural marriages to be dissolved. The Roman Catholic Church also allows the annulment of marriage (see unit 56).

CONTRACEPTION

Contraception (birth control) is any method used during sexual intercourse to avoid a pregnancy. The Roman Catholic and Anglican Churches disagree on methods of birth control. They do agree that:

- procreation is God's gift to the married couple

- God calls married couples to be responsible parents

- part of God's will is that children should be born within marriage

- sometimes it is acceptable to avoid bringing children into the world (for social, environmental, physical or psychological reasons).

However, the Churches do not agree on the methods of contraception.

The Roman Catholic Church

The Roman Catholic Church encourages couples to use the natural rhythms of the body and practise natural family planning if they want to have fewer children. This means a woman needs to be aware of her own fertile and infertile times. Artificial methods of contraception (condom, the coil, diaphragm, the Pill, sterilization, etc.) are not acceptable. Catholics teach that there must be loving union and procreation in all sexual intercourse. Artificial forms of contraception interfere with this.

The Anglican Church

The Anglican Church teaches that, while loving union and procreation should be present in marriage as a whole, the idea of procreation need not be present in every act of intercourse. Couples can use contraception, if both partners agree, and as long as they intend to have children at some stage in their marriage. Most other Protestant Churches agree with this view.

FACTFILE

Will it last?

In 1995 there were 192,000 first marriages in the United Kingdom. This was half the number of first marriages compared with 1970 and was the lowest figure since 1926. Altogether there were 332,000 marriages.

In the last twenty years, the proportion of marriages ending in divorce has risen from fifteen per cent to over twenty-five per cent. The UK now has the highest divorce rate in Europe.

The family is the ideal social unit

CHRISTIAN IDEALS

All Christians believe that the family is the ideal social unit. It is one of the 'building blocks' that help to keep society stable. They agree that:

- the family is part of God's plan for humanity

- families don't just happen. They need to be worked at

- marriage is a sacred agreement. To love takes effort, discipline and sacrifice. This applies to all relationships within the family

- the family is important in controlling the sex drive

- the family is a responsible unit for having and rearing children

- the family is where young people can learn about the customs, religion and traditions of society

- the family provides loving support for the young, the aged, the sick and the disabled.

The Church teaches that a person may have only one partner in marriage (monogamy). The Christian ideal family consists of a husband, wife and children, with close support for and from other members of the extended family, especially older relatives.

PARENTS AND CHILDREN

Christians expect children to honour their parents (see Exodus 20:12), even if they do not always obey them. Parents are not perfect and sometimes make mistakes. The ideal is that members of a family should be able to talk to each other about anything. Communication is essential. Good family relationships include love, mutual trust, co-operation, respect and tolerance.

Most parents are happy to see their children marry, but most Christians feel there is nothing wrong with remaining single. Some Christians believe that if people are homosexual (see unit 68) they have the right to have gay partnerships. Other Christians disagree.

Christian parents usually want to bring their children up as Christians. They have their children baptized and later confirmed (see unit 55). They may send their children to a church school. Others feel they don't want to force their own faith on their children. They hope that the children will make up their own minds as they mature (grow up). Parenting is an important part of family life, and Christians believe that being part of a loving family helps children to develop their own loving relationships.

Christian parents want their children to grow up with virtues such as respect for life, the ability to communicate with others, loyalty, generosity and the ability to form loving relationships. They would like their children to be able to think for themselves and to listen to others, to have respect for others (especially members of the opposite sex and the disadvantaged) and to take care of our planet.

SINGLE PARENTHOOD

Although they think it is better for children to have two loving parents, most Christians feel that single parenting is not always damaging

r children. Many Churches think that
ciety should do more to support single
arents. There should be cheaper housing
d better financial support. Absent parents,
e extended family and local communities
ould provide the emotional and moral
pport that single-parent families need.

HE OLDER GENERATION

some societies, older people are honoured
d respected. In the West, however, there
e many prejudices about old age, and
any elderly people are treated badly.

ney rarely live with their families. They
ther live alone or go into nursing homes.
any Christians think this is wrong. Elderly
eople have lots of experience and often
ve great wisdom and understanding. They
eserve more respect than our present
ciety gives them.

OMELESS FAMILIES

the UK there are about 500,000 homeless
milies, living in bed-sits or hostels. Much of
is type of housing is overcrowded and
healthy. Some is run by greedy landlords.
rug abuse, alcoholism, sexual harassment
d violence are common in these places.
nristian organizations such as the Children's
ociety (see units 26 and 64) and the
atholic Housing Aid Society (CHAS) try to
elp. They provide support, guidance and
gal help to homeless families. These
oups believe that:

all families have a right to adequate
housing

more houses at affordable rents should be
available for families on low incomes

the government should make more effort
to end the evils of homelessness.

THE VICIOUS CYCLE

Many Christians fear that rapid social change
is putting pressure on the traditional family.
They fear that a vicious cycle of

   family   →   social   →   family
breakdown   breakdown   breakdown

will lead to a total break-up of society as we
know it. They believe that more time should
be spent learning about personal and moral
issues in school. This is just as important as
learning 'facts' about different subjects.

FACTFILE

Parents on their own

The increase in the number of lone-
parent families in Britain in the last
twenty years has also meant that more
children now live in poverty. Only about
18% of lone parents work full-time,
and about 70% of lone parents and
their children live in poverty. Young girls
rarely have babies to 'get on the
council housing list'. Most lone parents
are alone because of the breakdown of
a relationship. Some have been
widowed. Nobody can expect to make
a fortune as a lone parent. In 1998
benefit rates were:

Lone parents (under 18)	£30.30
Lone parents (18 and over)	£50.35
Family premium	£11.05
Dependants	
(from birth to 11th birthday)	£19.80
Child benefit (eldest child)	£11.45
Child benefit (other children)	£9.30

So a lone parent with two children
below school age would receive a total
income of £101, excluding child
benefit payments which all parents
receive. Girls under sixteen are not
entitled to Income Support.

'Body language'

INTRODUCTION

The human sexual instinct is very powerful. It has been the subject of many taboos (rules about right and wrong). It is used to advertise everything from jeans to motor-cars.

PAST ATTITUDES

From St Paul onwards, the leaders of the Christian Church saw the sexual instinct as a threat to a person's religious life. The body was a trap, sexual pleasure a sin, and women were second-class citizens. Many leaders of the early Church thought it was their religious duty to reject the 'sins of the flesh'. They saw their physical and their spiritual selves as separate, fighting with one another. Until recently the Church saw sex as something bad that should only be practised within marriage.

SIN AND GUILT

For the past 2000 years, guilt has played a huge part in Christian thinking about sex. Priests and clergy of all Churches made ordinary men and women feel guilty about their natural sexual urges. They even told them that 'the sins of the flesh lead to the gates of hell'. People lived in fear, struggling with their sexual feelings in a confused and ignorant way.

Young people found this struggle almost impossible. After reaching puberty and the onset of intense sexual desire, many of them may have released their sexual tension by masturbation. The Church threatened these young people with the 'fires of hell'. This seems a long way from the loving message of the Gospels. Because of attitudes like this, the beauty and creative power of human sexuality were lost in a fog of fear and guilt.

Some Christian missionaries took their ideas about sexuality with them, to the people they went to convert. They did not see that these cultures already had their own teachings about sex. There, sexuality was accepted as a delightful fact of life, not something that was shameful. They had rules, not to repress the sexual urge, but rather to control and celebrate it for the good of all.

SEXUALITY TODAY

Attitudes to sexuality have changed over the last few years. The changes are not all for the good. Sex is big business and somehow the importance of human love has been set aside. Newsagents can now sell pornography that would have been banned a few years ago. Pornography is available on satellite television and on the Internet. More young people have sex before marriage. Thousands of young girls become pregnant every year. The number of cases of rape has increased. Sexually transmitted diseases, including AIDS, have reached epidemic levels round the world.

The Churches used to be the 'guardians of moral behaviour', teaching people what they considered to be right and wrong. Now, fewer people attend Church. The Churches have two choices:

- to adapt the Church's teachings to the needs of a changing world

- to keep on repeating their traditional teachings.

CELIBACY

For Christians, celibacy is 'the choice to remain unmarried to devote oneself completely to God'. When people join a monastery or a convent they make a public vow of chastity. The Roman Catholic Church in the West insists that its priests remain celibate. They base this on Matthew 19:10–12. Modern Catholics argue that priests should be free to decide whether or not to marry, as in the Anglican Church, but the Popes have ruled that priests must remain celibate.

FACTFILE

Sex statistics

A recent survey in the UK discovered that over 80% of people over 25 years of age were monogamous (had only one partner). Among 16–24 year-olds, 46% of men and 60% of women were monogamous. Only a small proportion had a large number of sexual partners. These were the ones most at risk from HIV/AIDS and other sexually transmitted diseases. They were also less likely to form permanent, lasting relationships later in life.

POINTS OF VIEW

Sexual intercourse is, first of all, a body language, through which couples … rejoice in each other's presence and the pleasure they exchange. For this they want to give thanks. Thus sex is a recurrent act of thanksgiving.

Second, because people want to make love repeatedly, they trust that their partners will respond to them again. So sex is also a recurrent act of hope …

Third, in the course of the day, couples hurt one another. Most of the hurts are forgiven and forgotten on the spot. But some … need a deeper level of love and communication to erase them. So sexual intercourse can also be an act of reconciliation.

Fourth, sexual intercourse confirms the sexual identity of the partners.

Finally, every time a couple makes love, they are saying to each other, 'I recognize you, I want you, I appreciate you.' … it is a recurrent act of personal affirmation.

… So sexual intercourse not only gives pleasure. It also has a powerful personal dimension in which the couple enrich one another's lives.

From this point of view marriage … provides a continuous, reliable and predictable relationship within which the rich potential of sex can thrive. … sex actually requires marriage for the realization of its potential.

… sex is so powerful and meaningful that justice can only be done to it in a continuous and enduring relationship.

(Jack Dominian – modern Roman Catholic theologian and psychiatrist)

Most people are afraid of death. One reason is that they don't know what is going to happen when they die. Fear of the unknown can be worse than fear of what is known.

KEY QUESTIONS

Is death the end? Do heaven and hell exist? Do we return to earth in another form? What is the soul?

Is death the end? Since the beginning of human history people have answered 'No!' Evidence from pre-history shows that people believed in some form of life after death. Today all world religions believe in life after death, although these beliefs may vary.

CHRISTIAN BELIEFS

Christianity teaches that God is loving and good. God cares for people. God wants to be close to them. This closeness can begin in this life, to be fulfilled after this life. Salvation is intended to make this personal relationship work. Christians believe that they keep their individual personality after death.

Christians also believe in judgement. They think that people will have to account for what they have done with their lives. The traditional teaching is that the good will be rewarded in heaven and the bad will be punished in hell.

Roman Catholics believe that only very good Christians will go straight to heaven. Most will go to purgatory – a kind of purifying process to prepare for heaven.

Many Christians reject the idea of hell, asking, 'How could a God of love create a place of eternal suffering?' They believe that heaven is being with God: hell is being apart from God. These are not places, but states of mind. Christians hope for eternal life because of the

'The Angel of Death' by Evelyn de Morgan (1890) based on the poem which she wrote as a teenager

The Angel of Death

Oh Love in Glory
With crowned brow
I feel thine arms
Around me now.
Soft thy kisses
Warm thy breath
Vision of love
Angel of death.

(Evelyn de Morgan)

death and resurrection of Jesus Christ. This 'eternal life' is not immortality, but is a continued state of being. Eternal life is eternal fellowship with God, which continues through life before death and life after death.

CHRISTIAN FUNERALS

Some Christians are buried in the ground; others are cremated. People attending funerals usually wear dark clothes. There is sadness about death, but the Christian funeral service stresses the hope that the dead person will be resurrected, in time. The service may include a reading of 1 Corinthians 15:51–55 which expresses this hope.

REFLECTION 1

H. Lovell of the United Reform Church, writes about the 'two deaths' that human beings have to undergo. The first death is the natural death of the body. The second death is death of the spirit. The second death is the punishment for sin. Christ's death on the cross means Christians no longer have to fear the second death because he took on himself the penalty for sin.

Now humans can begin to live a new life because they, too, can die to sin in their mortal life. God can help them to live lives free from sin. Their sinful nature is crucified and their new nature is raised from the dead.

The believer has already begun his new life in the Spirit … The whole matter is summed up for us in the words of Jesus … 'He that believeth hath eternal life.'

REFLECTION 2

It's a sleep,
Christ, life and death is a watch.
While the earth sleeps in loneliness
there on watch is the white moon;
there on watch is the Man,
Watching from the cross, while men
     lie asleep;
there on watch is the Man, drained of
     blood, the Man white
as the moon in the blackness of
     the night.

(Unamuno, 1864–1937 – Spanish poet)

FACTFILE

Sorrow and hope

Funeral services try to reflect both the sorrow of saying goodbye to a loved one and the hope of eternal life. The minister reminds the mourners of the Christian faith, in these words:

In the presence of death, Christians have sure ground for hope and confidence, and even for joy, because the Lord Jesus Christ, who shared our human life and death, was raised again and lives for ever. In him his people find eternal life, and … we put our whole trust in his goodness and mercy.

(*The Service Book of the Church in Wales*)

REFLECTIONS

Thinking about death

Your time here is short, very short; take another look at the way in which you spend it. Here man is today; tomorrow he is lost to view; and once a man is out of sight, it's not long before he passes out of mind. How dull they are, these hearts of ours, always occupied with the present instead of looking ahead to what lies before us! **Every action of yours, every thought, should be those of a man who expects to die before the day is out**. Death would have no terrors for you if you had a quiet conscience, would it? Then why not keep clear of sin, instead of running away from death? If you aren't fit to face death today, it's very unlikely you will be by tomorrow; besides … you have no guarantee that there will be any tomorrow – for you.

What's the use of having a long life, if there's so little improvement to show for it? … Unfortunately it happens, only too often, that the longer we live the more we add to our guilt. If only we could point to one day in our life here that was really well spent! Years have passed by since we turned to God …

Well for you, if you keep an eye on your deathbed all the time and put yourself in the right state of mind for death as each day passes …

Each morning, imagine to yourself that you won't last till evening; and when night comes, don't make bold to promise yourself a new day. Be ready for it all the time; so live, that death cannot take you unawares.

Plenty of people die quite suddenly, without any warning; the Son of Man will appear just when we are not expecting him … How bitterly you will regret all that carelessness, all that slackening of effort!

If you hope to live well and wisely, try to be, here and now, the man you would want to be on your deathbed.

(Thomas à Kempis, c.1379–1471 – monk. A few words and phrases have been altered.)

What is dying?

A ship sails and I stand watching till she fades on the horizon and someone at my side says, 'She is gone.' Gone where? Gone from my sight, that is all … and just at the moment when someone at my side says, 'She is gone,' there are others who are watching her coming, and … take up a glad shout 'There she comes!' and that is dying.

(Bishop Brent)

The secret of death

You would know the secret of death.
But how shall you find it unless you seek it in the heat of life?
The owl whose night-bound eyes are blind unto the day cannot unveil the mystery of light.
If you would indeed behold the spirit of death, open your heart wide unto the body of life.
For life and death are one, even as the river and the sea are one.
In the depths of your hopes and desires lies your silent knowledge of the beyond;

And like seeds dreaming beneath the snow your heart dreams of spring.

Trust the dreams, for in them is hidden the gate to eternity.

Your fear of death is but the trembling of the shepherd when he stands before the king whose hand is to be laid upon him in honour.

Is the shepherd not joyful beneath his trembling …?

For what is it to die but to stand naked in the wind and to melt into the sun?

And what is it to cease breathing but to free the breath from its restless tides, that it may rise … and seek God unencumbered?

Only when you drink from the river of silence shall you indeed sing.

And when you have reached the mountain top, then you shall begin to climb.

And when the earth shall claim your limbs, then shall you truly dance.

(Kahlil Gibran)

No trace of a shadow

Death is nothing at all. I have only slipped away into the next room. I am I, and you are you. Whatever we were to each other, that we still are. Call me by my old familiar name, speak to me in the easy way which you always used. Put no difference in your tone, wear no forced air of solemnity or sorrow. Laugh as we always laughed at the little jokes we enjoyed together. Play, smile, think of me, pray for me … Life means all that it ever meant. It is the same as it ever was … Why should I be out of mind because I am out of sight? I am waiting for you, for an interval, somewhere very near, just round the corner. All is well.

(Henry Scott Holland 1847–1918 – canon of St Paul's Cathedral)

A MESSAGE OF HOPE

Let us give thanks to the God and Father of our Lord Jesus Christ! Because of his great mercy he gave us new life by raising Jesus Christ from death. This fills us with a living hope.

(1 Peter 1:3)

FACTFILE

Life expectancy

The average life expectancy in Britain is 73 years for men and 78.5 for women. Married women and married men live longer than those who are single, widowed or divorced.

INTRODUCTION

In John's Gospel, Jesus says, 'My commandment is this: love one another, just as I love you.' (John 15:12) Jesus taught that religion is not just concerned with making people aware of God's rule on earth, it is about how we treat each other. Religion is about our relationships with others. The Churches believe it is part of their work to give people a lead on relationships.

All Christians believe that God created the universe. Therefore the universe, and all that is in it, has meaning. Christians believe that the Bible teaches that God gives people guidance about living in harmony. They believe that Jesus shows how God works in the world. In his earthly life, Jesus was concerned about the world and the people in it. Christians believe that this means they should follow his example and try to express God's will in the world today.

THE MODERN WORLD

Life today is very different from the way it was only a few years ago – and far, far different from how it was 2000 years ago. Modern technology brings many benefits, but it also raises many difficult questions. For example, what is right and what is wrong about nuclear power, chemical drugs, testing on animals, the role of the media, surrogate motherhood, test-tube babies, etc?

Life has changed so much that the Churches need to try to explain just what Christian moral standards are. Christians need this guidance. Therefore the Churches try to interpret the ideas in the Bible to give them meaning for today.

The Churches disagree about some moral and social issues, for example on birth control (see unit 57). Sometimes even within the same Church there is disagreement. For example, some Roman Catholic Christians do not agree with their Church's teaching about artificial forms of birth control. They argue that the world is already over-populated. Banning contraception could cause enormous numbers of deaths on earth.

Some Churches encourage their members to work out and apply their own moral attitudes in the light of Christian principles – to make their own decisions. Other Churches stress the importance of individual members remaining loyal to their own Church's authority and obeying its teachings on moral issues.

HOW DO CHURCHES DECIDE?

Churches have three sources of guidance:

- scripture (the Will of God as revealed in the Bible)

- tradition (the experience of the Church through Christian history)

- reason (human understanding and knowledge).

Churches emphasize the sources differently. They all take notice of what the Bible says, but interpret this in the light of their own traditional teaching.

They also pay attention to new ideas brought about from recent advances in human

Life has changed so much that the Churches need to try to explain just what Christian moral standards are

knowledge. All the Churches discuss the issues and give their members the chance to express their views. The final decisions are made by a representative body of some kind.

The Baptist Union of Great Britain

The Baptist Union would not wish to restrict the liberty (freedom) of individual congregations by making official statements on their behalf. However, the National Annual Assembly passes resolutions about a variety of issues. These need not be the opinion of every church, but they would still be the Baptist Union's general rule on social and moral matters. Baptists rely heavily on the Bible in making moral decisions.

The Church of England

The General Synod is the parliament of the Church of England. It meets three times a year and has 560 members, divided into three 'houses' – bishops, clergy and **laity** (non-ordained members). The Church relies equally on the Bible, tradition and reasoning.

The Roman Catholic Church

The Roman Catholic Church reaches decisions by looking at scripture, the tradition of the Church, the wisdom of its scholars and modern thinking in different parts of the Church throughout history. It sees scripture and tradition as inter-related. The Church issues statements through the Pope, the bishops and the Church's Councils, when the Church's teachings are made official.

The United Reformed Church

In the United Reformed Church the Bible is studied for all decision-making. The General Assembly meets once a year to take decisions on behalf of the whole Church. They reach decisions by majority vote, but 'recommend', 'encourage' or 'urge' their members, rather than giving them orders.

FACTFILE

But...

Jesus taught his followers to obey the law. He often quoted from the Ten Commandments. But there was always a 'but'. For example, 'You have heard it said "Do not commit adultery." But now I tell you: anyone who looks at a woman and wants to possess her is guilty of committing adultery with her in his heart.' (Matthew 5:27–8). He was really saying that people should not just obey the law, but look for the moral reason behind the law.

Jesus sometimes broke laws, such as the law forbidding work on the Sabbath. In doing this he showed that laws were a guide for moral behaviour, but that keeping the rules is not enough to make a person 'good'.

INTRODUCTION

All Christians believe that the universe, the world and everything in it have been created. They believe that our world is therefore sacred. This word means holy, special, precious, divine, worthy of respect and honour. Christians also believe that God made human beings to be like himself (Genesis 1:27) and that we are 'crowned with glory and honour' (Psalm 8:5). These teachings show that humans have a responsible task in God's plan for creation.

THE GREATEST COMMANDMENT

A teacher of the Law of Moses asked Jesus which commandment was the most important of all. Jesus replied that it was to love God with all your heart, soul, mind and strength. The second commandment was to love your neighbour as yourself. Love of God cannot be separated from love for humanity. Christians try to live their lives by this rule.

> We need to affirm the sacredness of all human life. Every person is somebody because s/he is a Child of God.
>
> (Dr Martin Luther King, 1929–68)

REVERENCE FOR LIFE

Many Christians go further, and say that people must try to love all of creation, not just human life. Albert Schweitzer (1875–1965) was a Christian medical missionary in Africa. He believed we must have a reverence for life. He wrote:

> Reverence concerning life is the greatest commandment … we take this so slightly, thoughtlessly plucking a flower, thoughtlessly stepping on a poor insect, thoughtlessly disregarding the suffering and lives of our fellow men and women.

Some Christians write about the way every living thing is unique. Thomas Merton (1915–68), a Trappist monk, wrote about this idea:

> No two created things are exactly alike. This particular tree will give glory to God by spreading out its roots in the earth and raising its branches into the air and the light, in a way that no other tree before or after it ever did, or will do… Each particular being in its individuality gives glory to God by being precisely what He wants it to be.

LOVE OF LIFE

> Lord, may we love all your creation, all the earth and every grain of sand in it. May we love every leaf, every ray of your light. May we love the animals … Let us not trouble them; let us not harass them; let us not deprive them of their happiness; let us not work against your intent. For we acknowledge unto you that … to withhold any measure of love from anything in your universe is to withhold that same measure from you.
>
> (Fyodor Dostoevsky, 1821–81 – Russian author)

'Reverence for all life is the greatest commandment'

ANIMALS

In the past, many Christians thought that animals were simply put on earth for human use. However, this is not what the Bible teaches. When God commanded that the earth should produce all kinds of animals 'He was pleased with what he saw,' (Genesis 1).

This means that humanity, at the top of the creation chain, has a responsibility for all creation. Through the ages many Christians have shown great concern for animals. St Francis of Assisi (1181–1226), the patron saint of animals, preached to the birds and tamed a wolf. William Wilberforce (1759–1833), who fought against slavery, also campaigned against bull-baiting and other blood sports. The Earl of Shaftesbury (1801–85) campaigned against vivisection (using live animals for experiments).

The RSPCA was founded by Christians. For over two centuries, many Quakers have been involved in animal rights. They were some of the first vegetarians. They also oppose fox-hunting and other blood sports.

In the past, the Churches have not had much to say about animal rights, but this has changed. The work of Greenpeace, the RSPCA, Animal Aid and the Worldwide Fund for Nature has inspired many Christians to speak out.

> Unnecessary and unjustifiable experiments and trials … should not take place. Intensive factory farming methods … are to be condemned. Every measure should be taken to preserve animal habitats.
>
> (Methodist Church statement, 1990)

In its report *Our Responsibility for the Living Environment*, the Church of England points out that Christians believe that animals were created by God. However, the value of animals is widely considered to be less that the value of human beings. Human beings are related to animals and have an obligation to them.

REFLECTION

Jesus is also a lover and pray-er of nature. Mountains, deserts, parks, lakes welcomed him for days at a time as he suffered his fame and his loneliness and his beauty and his decision-making in all these sacred temples. He chose the way and the lifestyle of the story teller, the parable maker who fashions a new creation out of the holy materials of the only creation we all share in common: the birds, the lilies of the field, the fish caught, the fig tree in bloom, the sheep versus the goats … His reverence for nature was so great that the creatures of nature were indeed his teachers and his professors.

(Matthew Fox)

FACTFILE

The Church's teaching about animals

Christians believe that the main causes of cruelty are avarice (greed for money), pride (contempt for nature) and unkindness. The search for profit leads to painful deaths in gin traps for millions of musquash, beaver and other animals. Whales, too, die painfully. It is people's unkindness that allows dog fights, animal baiting and other blood sports to continue.

In this unit we look at just a few of the social issues that concern Christians.

SUNDAY

In the UK the Law has recently changed to allow shops to stay open on Sundays. Many Christians believe this is wrong.

MONEY

In the UK five per cent of the population own 40 per cent of the wealth. To many Christians this seems unfair. In the reflection below the Salvation Army explains its views of money matters.

HOMELESSNESS

Many people in Britain live on the streets. Christians believe homelessness is a social evil. People become homeless for many reasons including poverty, problems at home, physical and sexual abuse, divorce, unemployment, mental illness, having a criminal record, alcohol or drug abuse, being a battered wife (or husband) and racism. Groups such as the Salvation Army, the Catholic Housing Aid Society and the Children's Society try to help the homeless and put pressure on the government to change its policies.

REFLECTION

In the early days of The Salvation Army much caring work was directed towards those who had little or no money …

William Booth, the Founder, was also concerned about man's 'unhealthy longing after wealth, house, lands, trade or any worldly thing for its own sake'. He felt that to desire money or position was good only if it was to be used to help others. The Bible teaches that stealing is wrong (Exodus 20:15) and that to covet is wrong (Exodus 20:17). The example of Jesus teaches us to put the needs of others before our own …

The Old Testament teaches the principle of tithing (Genesis 28:22). Many Salvationists allocate a tenth of their means to the needs of others in their corps, community and overseas. Others give more than a tenth …

Salvationists do not gamble because the main aim of a gambler is to gain at the expense of others … By avoiding games of chance altogether Salvationists guard against the problems and disappointments to which gambling so often leads. They are glad to support worthy charities … by giving donations rather than buying tickets.

High pressure advertising has resulted in a rapid increase in the use of store and credit cards and other means of obtaining credit … More and more people are falling into debt … Research carried out by the Freedom from Debt campaign has shown that debt is a major factor in marital stress and family breakdown. The NSPCC claims that debt is one of the three major factors in child abuse within the family.

… The Salvation Army in its early days frequently had converts who were suffering materially because they had mismanaged their money. Their acceptance of the Christian principles of thrift, honesty and temperance often raised their standard of living by a remarkable degree.

(The Salvation Army)

Wanted – a home

About 98,000 children and young people go missing in Britain every year. The law has double standards about the way abused children are treated. Social services and the police try to protect children who are abused at home or in care, but in 1993 the Children's Society discovered that runaways aged only fourteen were cautioned with soliciting. In law a girl under sixteen cannot give her consent to sex – yet girls under this age can be charged by the courts with soliciting.

The Children's Society believes that police and social services should give the same support and protection to young persons involved in street-sex as they do to any other child who has been sexually abused.

UNEMPLOYMENT

About three million people in Britain are out of work. The Church of England has this to say about unemployment:

> There are social and personal costs. Local communities decline; crime increases; individuals feel humiliated, angry and depressed; health problems increase; families suffer extra strain …

POINTS OF VIEW

- As long as there is poverty in the world I can never be rich, even if I have a million dollars. I can never be what I ought to be until you are what you ought to be.

  (Dr Martin Luther King, 1929–68)

- The earth belongs to everyone not just to the rich.

  (St Ambrose, 334–97 CE)

- Christianity began with a dreamer and ended up with a well-fed clergy.

  (Karl Marx, 1818–83)

- The love of money is the root of all evil.

  (1 Timothy 6:10)

FACTFILE

Fair wages?

At the same time that some three million people in Britain are without work, those in full-time work seem to be working longer hours. However, many workers work part-time, and nearly 83 per cent of female part-time workers said they did so through choice. Over 50 per cent of male part-time workers said they would prefer a full-time job.

Recent surveys of family incomes show that there is an ever-increasing gap between the 'haves' and the 'have-nots'. Top wage-earners used to receive eight times the lowest incomes. The figure has now increased to fifteen times.

INTRODUCTION

The law exists to protect the majority of people in society from the unfair actions of a minority. However, the law needs to be checked and updated to make sure that it is fair. Sometimes Christians and others have protested against unfair laws. This may mean breaking the old (unfair) law to put pressure on society to change it. One way of doing this is by non-violent direct action (e.g. Martin Luther King, see unit 16).

CRIME

People may commit crimes because they are bored, frustrated, angry or jealous, or just for the thrill of it. These are immediate causes. Deeper – underlying – causes may be poverty, poor housing, deprived upbringing, the desire to own more and spend more. In 1985 the Church of England report, *Faith in the City*, made the link between poverty and crime. It stressed that society today is too materialistic and people are encouraged to want more and more.

PUNISHMENT

There are five reasons for punishment:

- to protect (society/individuals/the offender from him/herself)

- to deter (put people off committing further crimes)

- to reform (try to make people better citizens)

Prison protects society

- to punish (retribution – 'an eye for an eye')

- to vindicate (crime is punished, so the law is protected).

Christians recognize that laws must exist to protect society, but they believe that the justice system should be merciful. An offender must be punished, but the sole aim of punishment is not retribution or revenge. They believe that any punishment should try to reform the offender.

Many Christians are involved in prison visiting, and work to help prisoners on release.

Britain punishes more people by sending them to prison than any other country in Europe. Many Christians believe that this system doesn't help prisoners, and many prisoners re-offend. The victim's needs are ignored. Christians believe there should be schemes where victim and offender can meet and try to understand each other, so that a healing process may take place.

POINTS OF VIEW

Punishment is useful only when it helps people to realize the hurt they are doing to ... themselves and others.

(Quaker viewpoint)

CAPITAL PUNISHMENT

Britain stopped using capital punishment (the death penalty) in 1970, but about 100 countries around the world still use it. The Churches have made public statements about it. One of the key questions is: Does it act as a deterrent? (Does it put people off committing murder?) Some people think that it does. When planning a crime, a criminal would think again if they thought their own life was at risk. Abolitionists (people who are against capital punishment) say that it is not a deterrent because murder is a 'crime apart'. Usually the whole purpose in planning a killing is to avoid being found out, so it is not a deterrent. Most Churches in Britain are against the death penalty. The Roman Catholic Church has not officially condemned it, but many bishops in Canada, the USA, France and Ireland have called for it to be abolished (done away with).

◇

FACTFILE

Prison reform

Many reforms that took place in the prison service began with the work of Elizabeth Fry (1780–1845), a Quaker. Elizabeth was active in the field of education and public services. She is best known, however, for her prison reforms. She began visiting women prisoners in the infamous Newgate Prison, teaching them to sew and reading the Bible to them. In 1817 she began her campaign to have the sexes separated in prison, and for women warders to supervise female prisoners. She also proposed that prisoners should be taught religious education and basic skills of reading and numeracy. Her report to the House of Commons committee played an important part in the introduction of new laws. Her motto was 'Charity to the soul is the soul of charity'.

QUOTES

- A deep reverence for human life is worth more than a thousand executions in the prevention of murder; and is, in fact, the great security for human life. The law of capital punishment while pretending to support this reverence does in fact tend to destroy it.

  (John Bright – first Quaker Member of Parliament, 1868)

- All human life is sacred and each human being, however wretched, can become a new person.

  (Salvation Army statement)

- For too long we have treated violence with violence and that's why it never seems to end.

  (Coretta Scott King – widow of Dr Martin Luther King, who was murdered)

- Perhaps the strongest argument … against the death penalty lies in the notion of redemption. Christianity professes that human beings are free either to follow the path of Christ or to stray from it and those who stray are sinners, but great stress is laid on the ability and duty of sinners to repent … After true repentance, a fresh start can be made in life. The death penalty … denies a … truly repentant criminal the chance to make the fresh start promised by Christ.

  (Amnesty International)

KEY WORDS

Prejudice – thinking badly of others without good reason; pre-judging someone without knowing them; a way of thinking about other groups of people.

Racism – an action or attitude that puts a particular racial group or person at a disadvantage. It can be defined as prejudice + power. It is also called racial discrimination. Sometimes racial prejudices may be supported by some key institutions in our society.

INTRODUCTION

It is mistaken to think of racism only in terms of strong personal prejudice, violence and racist organizations such as the British Movement. These are extremes. There are other, more general forms of racist thought and action that are more difficult to detect and to prevent.

Racist attitudes have been part of our culture for many centuries and this makes them difficult to shake off. These attitudes, for example, mean that in the UK, Asians are 50 times – and West Indians 36 times –

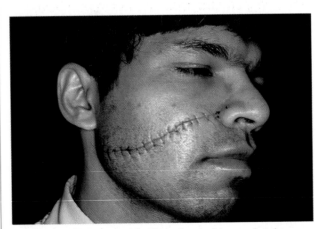

Asians are 50 times more likely than whites to be the victims of racial violence

more likely than white people to be victims of racial violence. People from ethnic minorities are four times more likely than white people to be homeless in London.

To survive racism, black people often learn to take pride in their blackness and refuse to be absorbed into a racist society. For example, the Rastafarian religion rejects white dominance. They think the West is full of evil, and hope eventually to return to Africa.

Some black Christians in the UK find that their community churches offer a sense of identity and security against racial discrimination.

Until recently the white, male-dominated mainstream Christian Churches have been racist. The missionary movement (see units 30, 32 and 75) was ignorant of black cultures. They forced people in Africa, the Americas, India and Australasia to accept a white, Christian world-view. As a result, ancient cultures disappeared. With modern forms of communication, people are now becoming aware of the richness of non-European cultures. People are also beginning to realize that all men and women are equal, and that we all live in one world. The mainstream Churches speak out against racism, discrimination and inequality. But we cannot be complacent: in the USA there are racist Churches, like the Church of Jesus Christ Christian Aryan Nations, that still teach white supremacy.

THE BIBLE AND RACISM

The modern Churches' attitudes to prejudice and discrimination are based on the Bible.

Creation: All human beings are made in the image of God (Genesis 1:26). Human beings are made for each other; to live together and to be responsible together for the whole of creation (Genesis 2:19–29). Unlike other creatures, there are no separate species within humanity. There is only one human race. What we call 'races' are only slight differences in the basic human stock (Genesis 3:20 and Acts 17:26).

Redemption: In Jesus Christ all barriers between humankind and God are broken down. Race, class, sex or status cease to be reasons for hostility and division (Galatians 3:28, Colossians 3:11, James 2:5–9).

QUOTES

- Guided by the Light of God within us ... we can all learn to value our differences in age, sex, physique, race and culture ... These are God's gifts.

  (Meg Maslin, quoted in *Quaker Faith and Practice*, The Religious Society of Friends, 1995)

- Every human being created in the image of God is a person for whom Christ died. Racism ... is an assault on Christ's values, and a rejection of his sacrifice.

  (World Council of Churches statement)

- **Definition**
  Racism results where prejudiced attitudes of superiority are combined with the power to shape society.

History
Western civilization is, and has long been, seriously flawed by racism.

Acknowledgement
British society nurtures racism through ... barriers which deny black people a just share of power and decision-making.

Confession
The church displays racism by failing to adapt so that black people can share fully in its life ... and its decision-making.

(*A Declaration on Racism* by the United Reform Church)

FACTFILE

Fair treatment for all

It is difficult to say how many of Jesus' early followers were black, since the Bible rarely describes people's outward appearances. There are many teachings about treating people fairly, however.

There is no difference between Jews and Gentiles, between slaves and free men, between men and women; you are all one in union with Christ Jesus.

(Galatians 3:28)

You must get rid of all these things: anger, passion, and hateful feelings. ... there is

no longer any distinction between Gentiles and Jews, circumcised and uncircumcised, barbarians, savages, slaves and free men, but Christ is all, Christ is in all.

(Colossians 3:8 and 11)

My brothers, as believers in our Lord Jesus Christ, the Lord of glory, you must never treat people in different ways according to their outward appearance ... if you treat people according to their outward appearance, you are guilty of sin, and the Law condemns you as a lawbreaker.

(James 2:1 and 8–9)

The Church is guilty of sexism

INTRODUCTION

Sexism is the opinion that one sex is not as good as the other, especially that women are less able in most ways than men. It is difficult to find out about how women in history have been treated, because societies have been dominated and ruled by men. This is called **patriarchy**. History, culture, language and religion have been patriarchal. Women were ruled by men and regarded as men's personal property. The Church has been guilty of sexism. This was because male church leaders interpreted the Old Testament in such a way that they kept the power of the Church for themselves (see unit 34).

THE OLD TESTAMENT

Women were treated as inferior because people chose to stress the idea that Eve was only in God's image because she was taken from Adam's spare rib. She was his 'helper'. People ignored the reading 'God created human beings … to be like himself. He created them male and female'. However, they never ignored the fact that the couple were banished from Eden because Eve first took the forbidden fruit from the serpent and then gave it to Adam (Genesis 3:1–24). In the story Adam had to work the soil, but Eve had a 'worse punishment'. 'I will increase your trouble in pregnancy and your pain in giving birth. In spite of this, you will still desire your husband, yet you will be subject to him.' The literal interpretation of Genesis says that, because of her biology, man must be master of woman.

At the time of Genesis, society was strictly patriarchal. Women were men's property. If a woman was raped, her father's or husband's property had been spoiled. Also women were thought to be 'unclean' when menstruating or after childbirth.

JESUS' ATTITUDES

Jesus always treated women with as much respect as men. They played an active part in his ministry. He first made himself known as the Messiah to a Samaritan woman (Matthew 4:7–30). The story of Martha and Mary shows he thought women were fit for other things besides housework (Luke 10:38–42). He appeared to women first after he rose from the dead (Matthew 28:1–10).

ST PAUL'S ATTITUDES

St Paul said 'there is no difference … between men and women; you are all one in union with Christ Jesus' (Galatians 3:28). He also said that a husband should love his wife as himself (1 Corinthians 7:3). But he warned wives to submit to their husbands (Ephesians 5:22). He also forbade women to teach in church 'or to have authority over men; they must keep quiet.' (1 Timothy 2:12).

CHRISTIAN HISTORY

During its 2000 year history, the Church has reinforced the general sexist attitudes that existed in society. Here is one example:

> Women should remain at home, sit still, keep house, bear and bring up children.
>
> (Martin Luther, 1483–1586

PORNOGRAPHY

Many Christians are deeply concerned about the way that sex is treated as goods for sale, and women are treated as less than human in pornographic books and films. Anna Grear, a Christian writer, explains why pornography is an insult to human dignity. The following section paraphrases her views.

To be human means to be a responsible, responsive being, rejoicing in all of life before the face of God. We are created, unique, valuable individuals.

She describes the way that pornography shows people as objects available for sale. They perform their sexual 'antics' at the press of a video remote control. She says that pornography destroys the 'whole nature of human personality'. It takes the personality out of a woman and reduces her to the outward, sexual parts. This 'dehumanizes' both the person being shown and the viewer. When we do not respect others as creations of God, we ourselves become less human.

The Bible stresses human relationships. This should help us to understand human sexuality better. The problem with pornography is that it does not emphasize sexuality enough! This is because it ignores relationships 'and restrains sexuality to the narrow confines of the genital. It has made sex trivial'.

In stressing genital sex, pornography makes sex shallow in meaning. 'It concentrates on the sexual act itself'. In doing this, the sex act is separated from the whole of human sexuality. The whole of what it means to be male and female is reduced to a mere difference in sexual anatomy.

Anna Grear believes that pornographic portrayal of women results in rape and violence. There is an increase in adultery and divorce. People believe that sexual freedom will bring them happiness. The results are that many children grow into 'adults incapable of forming lasting relationships themselves'. The degrading view of women in pop videos and advertising 'leads to men and boys despising women. The increasing use of younger and younger models cannot help but feed the problem of child abuse and incest. The circle is vicious and depressing.'

FACTFILE

Jesus and women

Jesus visited the home of Martha and Mary. Mary sat at Jesus' feet listening to him talking. Martha complained to him that she was left to do all the work and said, 'Tell her to come and help me!' Jesus replied, 'Martha, Martha! … Mary has chosen the right thing, and it will not be taken away from her.' (Luke 10:38–42).

On another occasion a woman who had suffered severe bleeding for twelve years touched Jesus' cloak, hoping to be cured. When she was found out, she was afraid and threw herself at Jesus' feet. Jesus said to her, 'My daughter, your faith has made you well. Go in peace.' (Luke 8:42–8).

Jesus even broke the Sabbath law to heal a woman's bad back. He placed his hands on hers and she stood up and praised God. (Luke 13:10–13)

137

INTRODUCTION

The psychologist Alfred Kinsey wrote a report on sexuality in the early 1950s.

QUOTE

There are not two discrete (separate) populations, heterosexual and homosexual … Only the human mind invents categories and tries to force facts into separated pigeon-holes.

(Alfred Kinsey – psychologist)

Kinsey concluded that each of us sits somewhere on a scale of sexuality, with total heterosexuality at one end and total homosexuality at the other. There are not two entirely separate kinds of sexual preference.

Nowadays homosexuals prefer the terms lesbian and gay because the word homosexual sounds like a doctor's diagnosis.

CHRISTIAN VIEWS

The campaign for lesbian and gay rights started in Europe and North America in the 1970s. This forced the Church and the rest of society to face the issues involved. Some Churches openly welcome lesbian and gay Christians. However, some homosexual Christians find it difficult to accept their own sexuality. 'Coming out' (admitting homosexuality) may be very difficult when family or friends believe homosexuality to be a sin. Lesbian and gay couples find it hard that they cannot marry their partner before God. Sometimes a sympathetic minister will arrange a ceremony of blessing.

WHAT THE BIBLE SAYS

There are six passages in the Bible that seem to talk about homosexuality.

POINTS OF VIEW

- No man is to have sexual relations with another man; God hates that.

    (Leviticus 18:22)

- …women pervert the use of their sex by unnatural acts… Men do shameful things with each other…

    (Romans 1:26–7)

Recently scholars have said that the way you translate different words depends on the attitudes you already have. For example, the Genesis passage says, 'Bring those men out … that we may know them.' The Hebrew verb 'to know' has always been taken to mean 'to have sex with'. Scholars point out that the word 'to know' is used 943 times in the Old Testament, and only ten times is it translated as 'to have sex with'. Yet this passage is often used as proof that homosexuality is condemned.

In Leviticus it says, 'No man is to have sexual relations with another man: God hates that.' As this is only addressed to men, does it mean that lesbianism is allowed? Christians who say that Jesus taught us to accept all people say that this verse should not be taken as a strict rule. They also point out that there is a rule in Leviticus that says that all divorced people who remarry should be killed!

The New Testament mentions homosexuality in the letters of St Paul. A recent theory suggests that in Romans, Paul is referring to men who have sex with male prostitutes. He may not be saying 'no' to all homosexual behaviour. This is open to argument. This passage is the only place in the Bible where lesbian sex is also condemned. But again, the meaning seems to change according to the translation used.

The verses in St Paul's other letters use Greek words that have always been given a homosexual meaning. But scholars of ancient Greek say that this was not a meaning that was usually given at the time Paul was writing. What was Paul actually trying to say? There were, after all, words in Greek for homosexual – but Paul didn't choose those words.

OPINIONS EXPRESSED BY CHRISTIANS

1 We should love the sinner but hate the sin.
2 We should accept people in a same-sex partnership because they are as valued by God as heterosexual people.
3 Homosexual acts are wrong; but we must treat homosexuals with understanding: the Church cannot exclude anyone.
4 No practising homosexual or lesbian should be rejected for ordination on grounds of their sexuality alone.
5 Homosexuality is evil and homosexuals are possessed by the devil.

TEACHINGS BY SOME CHURCHES

A Roman Catholic view

Tradition has always declared that homosexual acts are … contrary to the natural law. … under no circumstances can they be approved … They must be accepted with respect, compassion and sensitivity.

A Methodist view

For homosexual men and women, permanent relationships characterized by love can be an appropriate and Christian way of expressing their sexuality.

REFLECTION

I am a gay Christian. … I find that my life is a constant struggle between my faith and my sexuality. At times this conflict is unbearable. The Church's teachings are, without doubt, hypocritical. On the one hand, it publicly condemns homosexuality, bringing great suffering to Christians who are gay or lesbian – yet privately many of its leaders, including some of its bishops, are themselves homosexual.

… My partner and I have lived faithfully and happily together for twelve years. We love and care for each other very deeply. We have tried as best we can to live good, Christian lives. I am told that our love is wrong. How can … love between two human beings be wrong?

FACTFILE

God loves homosexuals

In 1998 the Anglican Church said that homosexuals 'are loved by God and that all baptized, believing and faithful persons, regardless of sexual orientation, are full members of the Body of Christ.'

INTRODUCTION

Disabled people have the same rights, feelings, needs and emotions as able-bodied people. They also need to develop real friendships with other people.

People sometimes use the terms 'impairment', 'disability', and 'handicap'. We should try to understand the differences between these words.

- Impairment is the effect of a disease, birth defect or injury upon the individual.

- Disability is the effect of the impairment on the individual's daily living.

- Handicap is the amount of social disadvantage suffered by the disabled person.

For example, a person may suffer a spinal injury in an accident – this is impairment. The effect of this is that they are unable to walk and are confined to a wheelchair – this is disability. There are some things they cannot do because of access and other problems – this is the handicap.

THE MENTALLY HANDICAPPED

In the past, people with mental handicaps were locked away in hospitals. This built up prejudice against them. Today, society is more aware that mentally handicapped people have plenty to offer and can develop within the community. However, because of lack of government money, many who are mentally ill are forced to live on the streets.

MARRIAGE AND DISABILITY

The Churches have debated whether disabled people should marry. This statement is a view shared by nearly all Christians:

> The disabled person needs to love and be loved. The disabled person needs to feel loveable. This basic need … is expressed in many ways: within family life, by a generous and trusting friendship and, in a unique way, between husband and wife in marriage. For some people a mental or physical handicap will exclude the possibility of such a relationship. But this must not be presumed. On the contrary, the natural right to marry must be respected unless the person concerned is clearly unable to understand what they are doing or unable to sustain the life-long commitment of marriage.
>
> … Serious consideration would have to be given to the implication of having children and caring for them. However, we must recognize the right of handicapped persons to enter marriage and the witness they can give to the beauty of married love.

(*All People Together*, a statement of the Roman Catholic Bishops of England and Wales, 1981

There may, of course, be some problems. For instance if one of the couple suffers from an incurable inherited disease which could be passed on to their children, should he or she be sterilized? However, it would be wrong to apply different standards to the marriages of disabled people than are applied to couples who do not have a disability.

REFLECTION

Jean Vanier works with the handicapped. Here he talks about L'Arche, the community that he founded.

Many things happen in our communities. There are crises of all sorts. Some people need good psychological help; some take a long time to find any peace of heart or healing. Some like to work; others hate it. There is joy, there is pain; it is the joy and pain of living together.

Most of the people we welcome are called to be with us all their lives. A few leave and get married. But the majority are much too severely wounded. Assistants come for periods of one or two years, and more and more are putting their roots down in the community. This is essential … But there are few people in society willing to climb down the ladder of success and become a brother or sister to a person with a mental handicap.

Our society sees the world in the form of a ladder: there is top and bottom. We are encouraged to climb that ladder, to seek success, promotion, wealth and power. At L'Arche, in living with our wounded brothers and sisters, we are discovering that to live humanly, it is not that ladder we should take as a model, but rather to see the world as a body …

People with a mental handicap are called to rise up in hope and to discover the beauty of their beings. Those who come to help are called to see what is most beautiful in their own hearts. And thus the body is formed. We discover we are linked together. … we learn to forgive each other … we become people of joy …

FACTFILE

Helen Keller, 1880–1968

Helen Keller became deaf and blind when she was only nineteen months old as a result of an illness. When she was about six years old her teacher, Anne Sullivan, began to spell words into Helen's palm while the child felt the objects with the other hand. She made no progress this way.

The breakthrough came when the teacher spelled the word 'water' while holding Helen's other hand under a pump. Suddenly it clicked in Helen's mind, and from that moment there was no looking back. Not only did she learn to speak her own language, but several others, too. She learned mathematics, Latin and Greek and went to university.

Her efforts to help handicapped people like herself gave encouragement to other blind and deaf people. She became one of America's best-known lecturers and authors.

By sheer determination, Helen Keller showed that her talents could be used not only for herself but for the benefit of others.

ABORTION

> **Abortion – a definition**
>
> - ending a pregnancy prematurely, before the foetus is able to survive, may be by an operation

The law

The 1990 Human Fertilization and Embryology Act allows abortion if the physical or mental health of the pregnant woman, or of any existing children, is at risk, or if there is a real risk that if the child were born it would be seriously handicapped. Abortion is not allowed after the 24th week of pregnancy.

Christian viewpoints

The key question for Christians is: When does life begin? The Roman Catholic Church says the human embryo must be treated as a human person from the moment of conception (when the sperm meets the egg). Roman Catholic teaching therefore does not allow abortion. The Protestant Churches believe that in some cases abortion should be allowed.

All Churches share the view that human life is sacred, and all humans have the right to live. They condemn the practice of abortion on grounds of mere convenience.

The Church of England view

The Church of England is against abortion in principle but accepts that each case is special. For example, it may be allowed when there is a risk to the mother's life, if the mother is pregnant because she has been raped, or there is a serious risk that a baby would be born handicapped.

We affirm that every human life, created in the divine image, is unique … born or yet to be born. We therefore believe that abortion is an evil … and that abortion on demand would be a very great evil. But … to withhold compassion is evil, and in … extreme distress or need, a very great evil … Christians need to face frankly the fact that … the 'right' choice is sometimes the acceptance of the lesser of two evils.

(Church of England Board for Social Responsibility, 1990)

The Roman Catholic view

The Roman Catholic Church teaches that the unborn child is a human, a gift from God and deserves respect as a human being with a right to life. They teach that to kill an unborn child at any stage is wrong. Even while it is tiny and hardly developed, the embryo or foetus is the beginning of a human life and life is God's gift. The teaching goes back to a second-century document, *The Didache*, which says 'You shall not kill by abortion the fruit of the womb.' Abortion should never be used as a means of birth control.

VOLUNTARY EUTHANASIA

> **Euthanasia – a definition**
>
> - to help someone who has a painful disease, that can't be cured, to die; sometimes called 'mercy killing'

In voluntary euthanasia, the person who is ill asks to die. Despite advances in modern medicine, dying can be a long and painful process. The law says that anyone (doctors included) who helps a patient to die risks being charged with murder or manslaughter.

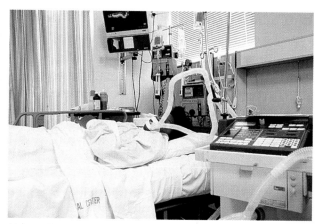

Hospital patient in intensive care

EXIT (the Voluntary Euthanasia Society) wants the present law to be changed. They believe that a person who is incurably ill should be allowed by law to have a painless death (if this is their expressed wish). They also believe that doctors should be allowed to help patients who can't be cured to die peacefully, provided the patient has signed a statement making their wishes known at least 30 days before.

Christian viewpoints

Most Christian Churches do not want the law to change. The Bible stresses that human life is sacred and a gift from God. In Ecclesiastes 8:8 it says 'no one has power over the day of his death'.

> Man does not have the right to end his own or another's life for the sake of avoiding possible suffering. ... God alone can determine when the power to take life should be given to man.
>
> (Dr Huw Morgan – GP and Christian)

> The argument for euthanasia will be answered if better methods of caring for the dying can be developed. Medical skill in terminal care must be improved ... The whole of the patient's need, including the spiritual, must be met.
>
> (Methodist Church statement, 1974)

KEY WORDS

Passive euthanasia – withholding life-saving treatment and allowing death to occur

Active euthanasia – giving a lethal dose of a drug to hasten death

FACTFILE

The Hippocratic Oath

For over 2000 years an ancient oath, the *Hippocratic Oath*, was taken by all doctors as they prepared to enter medicine. Many medical schools still impose a revised version of this oath when doctors graduate.

You do solemnly swear:

- that into whatsoever house you shall enter, it shall be for the good of the sick to the utmost of your power, holding yourselves far aloof from wrong, from corruption, from the tempting of others to vice

- that you will exercise your art solely for the cure of your patients and will give no drug, perform no operation, for a criminal purpose, even if solicited, far less suggest it

- that whatsoever you shall see or hear of the lives of men or women which is not fitting to be spoken, you will keep inviolably secret.

INTRODUCTION

There have been great advances in medical science. Doctors and scientists now have great power over life and death. This has created new moral problems. Here are some examples.

Artificial insemination by husband (AIH) – a husband's semen can be put into his wife using a special instrument.

Artificial insemination by donor (AID) – as above, but semen is provided by an anonymous donor, not the husband.

***In vitro* fertilization (IVF) or 'test-tube babies'** – the ovum (egg) is taken from the woman and fertilized by a man's semen in a laboratory. The embryo is then transferred to the woman's womb.

Egg donation – a woman donates an ovum that is fertilized by semen from a donor because both partners are infertile or carry an inherited defect.

Surrogacy – a woman bears a child for another woman who cannot become pregnant, then gives her the baby after birth.

Research on human embryos – may be simply to study early embryos or to test new methods or drugs on embryos.

HUMAN FERTILIZATION AND EMBRYOLOGY ACT 1990

This Act lists the following rules.

- A licensing authority, made up of medical and non-medical people, should be set up to oversee all work involving human semen, eggs or embryos.

- Donors of semen or eggs should remain anonymous. So should couples needing these services. Both partners must give written consent to treatment. No more than ten children should be born to one donor. A woman giving birth after egg or embryo donation should be regarded as the child's mother. The donor should have no rights or duties relating to the child.

- Frozen embryos can be stored for up to ten years. The embryo's parents have the right to decide on its use. If both parents die, that right should go to the storage authority.

- Surrogate (rent-a-womb) agencies should be banned.

- Human embryos should not be kept alive outside the womb more than fourteen days after they are fertilized. No embryo used for research can be transferred into a woman. Human embryos must not be put into the womb of another species.

The Church's view

Advances in the science of human fertilization have made the Churches think carefully about the moral issues involved. Not all Christians agree, even within the same Church.

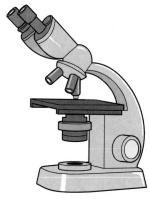

There have been great advances in medical science

A Roman Catholic view

The Roman Catholic Church is cautious about some aspects of *in vitro* fertilization. It says that as several eggs are fertilized, and spare embryos are thrown away or used for experiments, this means killing off human life. The Church has sympathy with couples who cannot have children. However, it thinks it is not right to treat the human embryo as 'experimental or as disposable material'. It also feels that conception involving a third person is wrong.

Anglican views

The Church of England Board for Social Responsibility wrote a paper on this subject in 1984. Not all Anglicans agree with its the views.

The majority of the Board agreed that AID was acceptable. Records must be kept; no more than ten children should be fathered by one donor; donors must not sell their sperm; on reaching the age of eighteen, the child should be allowed to know some details about the donor. The Board also said IVF should be allowed in cases of infertility and inheritable disorders.

The Board said surrogate motherhood should be illegal. They felt that 'bonding may take place between a woman and the child', so that she is unwilling to give it up. In 1988 the General Synod said surrogacy should not be protected by law.

The majority of the Board supported the idea that research should be allowed on embryos up to fourteen days old but the General Synod rejected this point.

A Methodist view

The Methodist statement of 1990 said, '... the important question is ... whose egg is fertilized by whose sperm.' It said, '... artificial insemination is acceptable provided the egg and sperm come from the baby's long-term parents.' It did not think AID was desirable.

KEY QUESTIONS

- When does life begin?
- Have embryos got rights?
- Have donors any rights?
- Who are the 'real' parents?
- Should humans interfere with God's creation?
- Do infertile couples have the right to use modern medical techniques to have children?
- Is sexual intercourse the only way humans should have children?

FACTFILE

Sarai and Hagar

The Old Testament mentions women who used surrogate mothers when they, themselves, couldn't have children. This one is from Genesis 16 and 21:

Abram's wife Sarai had not borne him any children. But she had an Egyptian slave girl named Hagar, and so she said to Abram, 'The Lord has kept me from having any children. Why don't you sleep with my slave-girl? Perhaps she can have a child for me.'

Hagar gave birth to a son Ishmael, and that was when the trouble started. First Sarai became jealous of her servant and treated her badly. Then, some years later, Sarai had a child of her own – and poor Hagar and her son Ishmael were sent away. The surrogate mother had no 'contract'!

A mother in Guatemala mourns the disappearance of her daughter, who was taken away from her by the state police

INTRODUCTION

Newspapers and television tell us that for some people every day is hell on earth. There are starving children, innocent victims of war, refugees struggling to survive amidst disease and death, prisoners locked up in filthy cells for speaking out against injustice, people living on the streets, child prostitutes, young women who are raped and tortured by prison guards. Their human rights are ignored.

Father Michael Evans works for Amnesty International. In the reflection opposite he explains why Christians should be actively involved in defending and promoting justice and human rights.

WORKING FOR HUMAN RIGHTS

Amnesty International works to free all prisoners of conscience. It wants to abolish the death penalty and to have fair trials for all political prisoners. Actions by Christians against Torture (ACT) works to abolish torture. If you want to get involved, you can write to these organizations (addresses on page 156).

FACTFILE

Terry Waite

In January 1987, Terry Waite, the special envoy of the Archbishop of Canterbury, became a hostage in Lebanon. He remained captive for 1763 days. He was blindfolded, in chains and alone. He was beaten and tortured. As his ordeal began he made three resolutions: no regrets, no false sentimentality, no self-pity.

REFLECTION

Human beings are special because God made them. They are made in the image and likeness of God and therefore have dignity and human rights.

It is not just a matter of dignity and human rights. Human beings are all members of one single human family. They share life with each other and with their Creator. In a mysterious way, humans are bound up together so that **whenever one human being is made to suffer, the rest of humanity suffers too and is weakened and threatened**. St Paul wrote about the Christian community as a single living body. This is true also of the whole human race. We shed our own blood if we hurt others. Torture and oppression are suicidal for humanity. **We allow our own freedom to be whittled away if we sit back while others are deprived of liberty. No one is an island**. The deep invisible bonds between all human beings everywhere mean that wherever human rights are violated, we ourselves are violated. You could say that **the violation of human rights is a violation of God.**

God is the One who brings justice to the oppressed, the Lord who sets prisoners free, the Lord who lifts up those who are bowed down (Psalm 146).

God is also the One who demands justice, as we can see from the writings of the prophets in the Bible who spoke out against oppression. Their challenge is thrown down not only to the rulers of their day, but also to God's people now. **It is nonsense to talk of loving others if we do nothing practical to lift them out of their poverty, degradation and oppression.**

God is also the One who promises justice. Gradually the Bible speaks of the hope of an Anointed One, the Messiah, who is filled with the Spirit. He is sent to bring good news to the poor, to bind up hearts that are broken, to proclaim liberty to captives and freedom to those in prison (Isaiah 61).

Jesus was not only the promised Messiah but actually God in person, made flesh and living among us. The Son of God experienced arrest as a political agitator. He was beaten, tortured, humiliated and executed though he had done nothing wrong. **In the person of Jesus Christ, God has become a brother in the human family, the neighbour of every human being**. By means of the Resurrection he is now able to be present to everyone everywhere. He takes personally whatever is done to anybody else! That is perhaps one meaning of those words of Jesus, that whatever we do for the least of his brothers and sisters, we do for Jesus himself. And that whatever we fail to do for them we fail to do for him (Matthew 25:31ff). This applies in a special way to our commitment to the poor and oppressed. These are the people with whom Jesus specially identified.

We cannot allow ourselves to 'pass by on the other side'. **We have to be the Good Samaritan, stopping and giving practical help** – by writing a letter, sending a telegram or signing a petition.

(Adapted from an article by Father Michael Evans of Amnesty International)

THE STATE OF THE WORLD

The richest people (The North)	The poorest people (The South)
• $573 spent on health per person	• Only $2 spent on health per person
• 79% of population have toilets	• Only 9% have toilets
• 98% of women and 99% of men can read	• 29% of women and 55% of men can read
• 18 in every 1000 children die before they are 5	• 176 in every 1000 children die before they are 5

FACTS OF DEATH

- Every day 35,000 people die from hunger.

- More money is spent on arms in one day than the world's two billion poorest people live on in one year.

- In the six years from 1993 to 1999 more people died from hunger than died in all wars, revolutions and murders in the last 150 years.

Many things link together to cause world poverty: the arms trade, unfair trading conditions, big business interests, super-power struggles, overpopulation, exploitation by Europeans, the cycle of debt. Poor countries need cash to develop their economies, so they borrow money from the World Bank and the International Monetary Fund (IMF). These organizations charge huge amounts of interest, which only makes matters worse for the poor countries of the South.

Two Christian organizations that work for the world's poor are Christian Aid and the Catholic Agency for Overseas Development (CAFOD). Many Churches also try to put pressure on the governments of the rich countries to change their unfair policies.

CAFOD

CAFOD believes that all people are equal in the sight of God. It raises money for projects such as production of food, water supplies, medicine and education. People in Britain can be linked with people in Africa, Asia and Latin America. CAFOD groups work in schools or parishes to raise funds to support self-help schemes for the world's poor.

CHRISTIAN AID

Christian Aid helps the poor and powerless by giving them the power to help themselves. It tries to work as partners with the poor. It works in over 70 countries, with more than 500 partner organizations, including Catholic groups. Christian Aid also works in emergency areas and pays for medical supplies, food and blankets, transport and building materials. It tries to support, feed and resettle refugees.

Why do Christians get involved?

- Christians believe that God loves the world and everything in it. They believe that God became human in Jesus and that they meet God in every human being.

- Christians try to follow the example of Jesus in the ways he mixed with and showed respect for the poor and despised.

- Christianity teaches justice and equality, treating people with compassion and respect.

- Christianity provides a vision of what life could be like if everyone became less self-centred.

- For many Christians, faith is not a private matter, it must be put into action.

A Church that cares about the poor can never be a wealthy Church

OVERPOPULATION

Every day about 2.5 million people are born into the world. It took 10,000 generations for the world population to reach two billion, but it is taking only one generation to leap from two billion to ten billion.

Overpopulation causes great problems. The Roman Catholic Church refuses to allow artificial methods of birth control. They say the answer is to share out wealth not contraception. Other Christians disagree with the ban on contraception. Without contraception, they say, the world is heading for disaster.

QUOTE

What is needed is ... that the rich should no longer dictate to the poor countries the terms on which they will trade with them.

(Baptist Church statement, adapted)

POINTS OF VIEW

A Church that is in solidarity with the poor can never be a wealthy Church. It must sell all ... It must use its wealth and resources for the sake of the least of Christ's brethren.

(Archbishop Desmond Tutu)

FACTFILE

Christian Aid and world poverty

The following poem lies behind Christian Aid's policy of helping poor nations to help themselves:

If you give a man a fish, he will eat once.

If you teach a man to fish, he will eat for the rest of his life.

If you are thinking a year ahead, sow seed.

If you are thinking one hundred years ahead, educate the people.

By sowing seed, you will harvest once.

By planting a tree, you will harvest tenfold.

By educating the people, you will harvest one hundredfold.

(Kuantzu)

149

THE 'JUST WAR'

Although they believe that killing is wrong, many Christians think there can be a 'just war'. This is a war they think is morally right. St Thomas Aquinas (1225–74) set out three conditions for a just war. Two more rules were added later:

1 The war must be started and controlled by the government or ruler of a country.

2 There must be a good cause; those who are attacked must deserve to be attacked.

3 The war must be fought to bring good or to avoid evil. Peace and justice must be restored afterwards.

4 The war must be the last resort; all other possible ways of solving the problem must have been tried first.

5 There must be 'proportionality' in the way the war is fought (e.g. to bomb a whole village for sheltering an enemy in one house is wrong). Civilians must not be killed. Only the amount of force needed to win must be used

THE 'HOLY WAR'

People fight holy wars because they believe that God is on their side, or they feel that they have righteousness on their side. The Crusades in the eleventh and twelfth centuries were holy wars. These were fought against the Turks to free the holy places of Palestine from the Muslims. The Christian Church identified the Muslims with Satan, and the Crusaders with God. The Muslims thought their wars were holy too. Such wars are very violent because the people who fight in them are stirred up by their religion.

The idea of a holy war poses many questions:

- Who really knows what is right?

- Is it right to kill for religion?

- How can anyone know that God is on their side?

WAR AND PEACE

Jesus said, 'You are going to hear the noise of battles close by and the news of battles far away … Countries will fight each other …' (Matthew 24:6–7).

The largest and bloodiest wars in history were fought in the twentieth century. Millions of men, women and children died from war.

In Matthew 5:9, Jesus says, 'Happy are those who work for peace; God will call them his children.' Jesus taught about peace, but Christians are divided about whether it is ever right to fight in a war or to use violence.

Some believe there are times when a Christian has no choice. This is because they believe that not fighting will be much worse. For example, the German theologian, Dietrich Bonhoeffer (1906–45) took part in an assassination plot against Hitler. He was prepared to give up his life and his principles to try to rid the world of Nazism. The plot failed and Bonhoeffer was executed.

WEAPONS OF MASS DESTRUCTION

Chemical, biological and nuclear weapons are 'weapons of mass destruction'.

The arms trade is one of the evils of our time

Il Churches condemn the use of these eapons, and the continued testing of them.

Though the monstrous power of these weapons act as a deterrent, it is to be feared that the mere continuance of nuclear tests undertaken with war in mind, will have fatal consequences for life on earth. ... the arms race should cease ... nuclear weapons should be banned.

(Roman Catholic teaching, *Pacem in Terris*)

ACIFISM

onscientious objectors are people who refuse fight in a war because of their conscience. any of these are pacifists, people who totally ppose war and violence. The Religious ociety of Friends are pacifists. They are spired by the *Peace Testimony*, which they st presented to Charles II in 1660.

We utterly deny all outward wars and strife, and fighting with outward weapons, for any end, or under any pretence whatever; this is our testimony to the whole world. The Spirit of Christ is not changeable ... and we ... testify to the world, that the Spirit of Christ, which leads us into all truth, will never move us to fight and war against any man with outward weapons, neither for the kingdom of Christ, nor for the kingdoms of the world.

THE ARMS TRADE

ountries such as the UK, France and the SA sell weapons to other countries, making uge profits. Many Christians believe this is vil. Spending money on arms is one of the ajor causes of world poverty.

POINTS OF VIEW

We used to wonder where war lived, what it was that made it so vile. And now we realize ... that it is inside ourselves.

(Albert Camus, 1923–60 – writer)

REFLECTION

Peace is what I leave with you; it is my own peace that I give you. I do not give it as the world does. Do not be worried and upset; do not be afraid.

(John 14:27)

FACTFILE

The peace rose

In June 1939 rose-growers from many countries were admiring a beautiful new rose, developed by Francis Meilland in France. The rose was not named and was known only as number 3–35–40. When war broke out three months later, Meilland sent small parcels of budded 3–35–40 to rose-growing friends.

They arranged a name-giving ceremony for 29 April 1945. 'We think this greatest new rose of our time should be named for the world's greatest desire – PEACE.' By coincidence, this was the day that Berlin fell to the Allies – and marked the beginning of peace in Europe.

Christianity is still a missionary religion (see unit 30). In the past it tried to convert the 'first peoples' of the world – the original inhabitants of the lands. Missionaries often knew little of the cultures of the people they were trying to convert. The article 'The sword and the cross' below describes some of the effects the early missionaries had.

Many modern-thinking Christians now believe that missionary work should not be about getting people to join a religious group (proselytizing). It should be about witness (showing what Christianity is through work). In the Dialogue opposite, two monks, Brother David and Brother Thomas, talk to physicist Fritjof Capra about modern ideas of mission.

FACTFILE

'Your poverty is greater than ours...'

Mother Teresa wrote this to the rich countries of the world:

The spiritual poverty of the West is much greater than the physical poverty of the East. In the West there are millions of people who suffer loneliness and emptiness, who feel unloved and unwanted. They are not the hungry in the physical sense; what is missing is a relationship with God and with each other.

THE SWORD AND THE CROSS

The first Indian bishop of the Peruvian Methodist Church, Pablo Mamani Mamani says, 'the Spanish tried hard to destroy Inca culture and religion. The Church was not interested in anything but our gold and our land. For nearly 300 years the Catholic Church did nothing to help the indigenous people [the original inhabitants]. What's worse, they worked hand-in-hand with the invaders who killed millions of people.'

A Catholic priest was put in charge of most Andean villages. The Church confiscated land from local people and forced them to work the fields without pay.

The Spanish began to lose power in the early nineteenth century. Church officials asked that land taken illegally from local communities be turned over to the Church. As a result, when the country became independent in 1824 the Catholic Church became the largest land-owner in Peru.

Today, in Lima, the Church owns some of the worst slums. Priests recently built a wall around their property to prevent poor peasants from invading. The Dominican Fathers, who own most of the slum housing recently raised rents to $35 a month. (The minimum wage in Peru is $54 a month.)

The Reverend Enrique Minaya says that for nearly 500 years the churches have worked with governments to keep the white rulers in their place.

Peruvian liberation theologian Gustavo Gutierrez echoes Minaya. He stresses that we must honestly accept what the 'discovery' of the Americas meant for indigenous people. He says, we must not copy those who want to hide the way that native peoples and their culture have been destroyed.

(Lucien Chauvin, adapted)

Peruvian prayer: a blend of Christianity and tradition

DIALOGUE

David: Missionary work used to be almost about competition, expansion, domination, of masculine emphasis on quantity – how many can we baptize in a hurry?

Fritjof: And what is mission now?

David: … There are very few missionaries today who would try to turn the clock back. Basically witness is the key word today, not proselytizing.

Thomas: Witness and dialogue … our presence among these people and their religions, especially in Asia, is a presence of dialogue.

Fritjof: So the aim of mission is no longer to convert people to Catholicism?

Thomas: No. In fact it never was. The missionary's aim is to be a witness to the good news of God's universal plan of salvation. 'Conversion' is not something the missionary does; it is uniquely the action of God within the heart of one who realizes, 'This is good news for me!'

David: There are now whole missionary groups who go into places where they will not make converts.

Thomas: One religious order's mission explicitly excludes preaching, converting, baptizing, and that is the Missionaries of Charity of Mother Teresa. Her mission was exclusively the work of love. … she wanted her sisters to witness to their faith solely through prayer and the works of love.

Fritjof: What does that mean: 'to witness to their faith'?

Thomas: To make known their faith … above all by living it. You see the difference between witnessing and preaching … is that witnessing is not projected through my ego. … I am simply present in order to let a great truth shine through me. …

David: Please know this is not a cunning way of getting others to sign up as Christians. It is simply a witness to our common humanity. That witness is always needed. … In this context, mission means that you give witness to human dignity as Jesus did. … To do this remains the task of Christian mission.

Fritjof: Now for somebody like Mother Teresa or any of these missionaries who do not preach and do not baptize, what is their purpose in witnessing in Asia or Africa? Why not do it right here?

David: They do it right here, too. They do it everywhere.

Fritjof: And they call themselves 'missionaries' also here?

David: Missionaries means simply 'people who are sent'. According to the Gospels, Jesus sends out his disciples because they are full of enthusiasm for the new life he opens up for them. …

Fritjof: So why would you be sent to Thailand as a Catholic missionary?

David: You may be sent anyplace where there is oppression, exploitation, human misery.

(Fritjof Capra, *Belonging to the Universe*, Penguin Books, 1992)

Mother Earth is dying

- In the last 25 years the number of babies born with serious defects has doubled.

- Tropical rainforests half the size of California are destroyed every year.

- Britain has more motor vehicles today than it had people in 1871.

- Every day 72 square miles of new desert appear on earth.

- During 1988–91 pollution in British rain increased by 23 per cent.

- Nearly half of Britain's scientific research is devoted to war.

- If today is a typical day, we will lose 40 to 100 species – for ever.

Mother Earth

In recent years pressure groups such as Greenpeace have raised awareness about problems such as global warming, CFCs, the ozone layer, acid rain, nuclear accidents and polluted seas.

CHRISTIAN RESPONSES

Christianity teaches that God created the earth, and human beings are the stewards (managers) of creation. Human beings should work with nature, to protect what has been given to them. However, greedy people exploit nature for gain. Multinational companies exploit the earth's natural resources. They don't care about the damage they cause.

Greedy people often interpret the teachings of the Bible to suit themselves. They claim that God gave humans the right to exploit nature. They claim this is what the creation account in the Book of Genesis means. Yet it does not say that people should exploit creation. Instead it says that human beings should 'bring it under control' (Genesis 1:28)

Christians have begun to speak out about the environmental crisis:

> [We] are to be stewards and curators, no exploiters, of [the earth's] resources. Christians must support those working for the development of more appropriate sustainable lifestyles.
>
> (Methodist Conference statement, 199

POINTS OF VIEW

- The earth is ... mother of all that is natural, mother of all that is human. She is mother of all, for contained in her are the seeds of all.

  (Hildegard of Bingen)

- Already the human race has begun to feel the effects of the wounds that we have inflicted on mother earth. We have begun to put our hands in her lanced side and in her crucified hands and feet ... Mother Earth is dying. ... [Are we] involved in a matricide that is also ecocide? Are we being kept in the dark about it by our media, government officials, and educational and religious institutions?

  (Matthew Fox)

The earth and all life on it is a gift from God for us to share and develop not to dominate and exploit.

(Roman Catholic statement, 1991)

REFLECTION

We seem to be at a turning point in human history. We can choose life or watch the planet become uninhabitable for our species. Somehow I believe that we will pass through this dark night of our planetary soul to a new period of harmony with the God that is to be found within each of us and that S/He will inspire us to use our skills, our wisdom, our creativity, our love, our faith – even our doubts and fears – to make peace with the planet.

(Pat Saunders, a Quaker)

KEY QUESTIONS

Shouldn't we use our power over nature in a responsible way?
How can we see the difference between need and greed in our own lives?
How can we, as individuals, stop Mother Earth from dying?

Canticle of the Sun

This prayer by St Francis of Assisi gives thanks to God for the beautiful world.

O most high, almighty Lord God,
  to you belong praise, glory, honour,
  and all blessing!
Praised be my Lord God
  for all his creatures,

especially for my brother the sun,
  who brings us the day and
  who brings us the light; fair is he
  and shines with a very great splendour;
  O Lord, he signifies you to us!
Praised be my Lord for our sister the
  moon, and for the stars which he has
  set clear and lovely in heaven.
Praised be my Lord for our brother the
  wind, and for the air and clouds,
  calms and all weather by which you
  uphold life in all creatures.
Praised be my Lord for our sister water,
  who is very serviceable to us …
Praised be my Lord for our brother fire,
  through whom you give us light in the
  darkness; …
Praised be my Lord for our mother
  the earth, who sustains us and keeps
  us and brings forth various fruits and
  flowers of many colours, and grass.

FACTFILE

'He made me!'
In his book *Confessions*, St Augustine describes his search for God.

'What is this God?' I asked the earth, and it answered, 'I am not He,' and all things that are in the earth made the same confession. I asked the sea and the deeps … and they answered, 'We are not your God, seek higher …'

I asked the heavens, the sun, the moon, the stars … And I said to all the things that throng the gateways of the senses … and they cried out in a great voice 'He made us.' I asked the whole frame of the universe about my God and it answered me, 'I am not He, but He made me!'

155

SOME IMPORTANT ADDRESSES

Actions by Christians Against Torture
32 Wentworth Hills
Wembley Middlesex HA9 9SG

Amnesty International
99–119 Rosebury Avenue
London EC1R 4RE

Anglican Society for the Welfare of Animals
10 Chester Avenue
Hawkenbury
Tunbridge Wells, Kent TN2 4TZ

Baptist Union of Great Britain
Baptist House
PO Box 44
129 Broadway
Didcot
Oxon OX11 8RT

CAFOD (Catholic Fund for Overseas Development)
2 Romero Close
Stockwell Road
London SW9 9TY

Catholic Housing Aid Society
209 Old Marylebone Road
London NW1 5QT

Catholic Truth Society
192 Vauxhall Bridge Road
London SW1V 1PD

The Children's Society
Edward Rudolf House
Margery Street
London WC1X 0JL

Christian Aid
PO Box 100
London SE1 7RT

Campaign for Nuclear Disarmament
162 Holloway Road
London N7 8DQ

ChildLine
Royal Mail Building
50 Studd Street
London N1 0QW

Church Action on Poverty
Central Buildings
Oldham Street
Manchester M1 1JJ

Community and Race Relations Unit
Council of Churches in Britain and Ireland
Inter-Church House
35–41 Lower Marsh
London SE1 7RL

Lesbian and Gay Christian Movement
Oxford House
Derbyshire Street
London E2 6HG

The Methodist Church
1 Central Buildings
Westminster
London SW1H 9NH

Peace Pledge Union
41b Brecknock Road
London N7 0BT

Quakers (The Religious Society of Friends)
Friends House
173–177 Euston Road
London NW1 2BJ

The Salvation Army
Territorial Headquarters
105–109 Judd Street
London WC1H 9TS

The United Reformed Church
86 Tavistock Place
London WC1H 9RT

If you want information from any of these sources:

- state clearly what information you want and why you want it
- always send a stamped, self-addressed envelope
- look in your telephone directory for local organizations.

GLOSSARY

Absolution a priest telling someone their sins are forgiven

Adoration feelings and actions that show love God

Advent a time of preparation for the coming of Jesus, during the four weeks before Christmas

Agape Greek word meaning 'love'

Altar holy table where the Eucharist is celebrated

Amen 'let it be', said at the end of prayer

Anglican a member of the Church of England or a Church in partnership with that Church

Annulment setting aside of a marriage

Annunciation the time when the Angel Gabriel told Mary she would give birth to the Messiah

Apocalypse writings that describe the end of the world

Apocrypha 'doubtful' books of the Old Testament

Apostle one of Jesus' first twelve followers; St Paul took the place of Judas

Ascension when Jesus went up (ascended) into heaven

Atonement the healing of the relationship between God and human beings, brought about by Jesus

Awe feeling of wonder, fear, reverence

Baptism the sacrament in which people 'enter' the Church

Baptistry a building or special pool for believers' baptism

Beatitudes the nine blessings Jesus gave in the Sermon on the Mount (Matthew 5:1–12)

Bible the holy book of Christians

Canonization making somebody a saint

Catechism a series of questions and answers used by the Church to teach

Chalice cup used for wine of Holy Communion

Christ Anointed One, Chosen One, Messiah

Christmas festival celebrating Christ's birth

Chrismation ceremony in the Orthodox Church which takes place after baptism

Church the whole Christian community; a place where Christians meet

Confession admitting your sins and asking for forgiveness

Confirmation ceremony where baptized Christians confirm their faith

Congregation gathering of people for worship

Consecrate make something holy

Creed a statement of belief

Crucifixion being nailed to a cross – form of capital punishment used by the Romans

Deacon assistant to a priest

Dedicate make a person or building sacred to God

Denomination a group of churches with their own particular traditions

Diocese a district of a Church controlled by a bishop

Disciple a follower of Jesus

Dissolution Roman Catholic equivalent to divorce

Easter festival celebrating Jesus rising from the dead

Ecumenical 'worldwide'; bringing the Churches together

Epiphany the showing of Jesus as the Son of God

Epistles letters in the New Testament

Eucharist 'thanksgiving' using bread and wine as symbols of the body and blood of Christ (also called Holy Communion, Mass, the Lord's Supper)

Evangelism spreading the Christian message

Faith an inner belief and trust

Fall the story of how Adam and Eve offended God

Font a bowl used to baptize infants

Fundamentalist someone who believes the Bible is literally (word for word) true

Genuflection going down on the right knee as a sign of respect to God

Gospels 'good news'; first four books in the New Testament

Grace the loving help of God

Heretic somebody who has different beliefs from the Church's teaching

Holy Spirit the power of God

Holy Week the week before Easter

Hymn religious song that the congregation sings together

Icon special picture of Christ or a saint, used to assist worship

Immaculate conception how Mary conceived Jesus without sexual intercourse

Incarnation when God became a human person in Jesus

Infallible 'without error'; usually refers to the authority of the Pope

Inquisition persecution of heretics by the Roman Catholic Church begun in the thirteenth century

Lay/Laity ordinary Christians who are not ordained

Lent the 40 days before Easter

Liturgy worship that follows set rules

Martyr 'witness'; someone who died for their faith

Mass Roman Catholic name for the Eucharist

Messiah the anointed or chosen one

Minister the person in charge of a Free Church, or to look after and care for

Mission the work a person believes s/he has been sent into the world to do

Monotheistic believing in one God

Ordination ceremony which makes a person a church leader

Original sin the sin of Adam (humankind) that no one in the world can escape from

Orthodox The eastern Churches that broke away from Rome in the eleventh century

Parable a story with an outer and an inner meaning

Pater Noster the Latin words for 'Our Father'

Patriarch leader of the Orthodox Church

Patriarchy a society ruled by men

Penance an act to show sorrow for one's sins

Pentecost Jewish festival when the early Christians received the Holy Spirit

Pilgrim somebody who goes on a religious journey

Pope title given to the leader of the Roman Catholic Church

Priest ordained minister who is authorized to perform religious ceremonies

Pulpit a raised platform from where sermons are given

Purgatory a state between heaven and hell where people are prepared for heaven

Redeemer a saviour or liberator

Redemption freedom (from sin); Christians believe Jesus obtained salvation through his death and resurrection

Reformation sixteenth-century movement to reform the Roman Church which marked the beginning of the Protestant Churches

Resurrection when Jesus is believed to have risen from the dead

Reverence a deep love; an awareness of holiness

Rituals actions that carry meaning in religious worship

Rosary a set of prayers, using a string of beads which honours the Virgin Mary

Sacrament an outward, visible sign of an inward, invisible blessing, obtained through certain rituals

Sacred holy; places, people and things made holy by God's power

Salvation wholeness; the healing of the broken relationship between God and humanity

Sanctification making holy

Scripture the sacred writings of a religion; for Christians this is the Bible

Sermon talk or message given by a church leader

Shrine small place of worship, or especially holy place, usually connected to a special religious event or person

Sin literally 'to miss the mark'; wrong attitude of self-centredness

Tabernacle altar or shrine

Transcendent something that is above, beyond and free from the limitations of this world

Transfigure change in appearance, especially the change in Christ's appearance as described in the Gospels

Transubstantiation Roman Catholic belief that during the Mass the bread and wine mysteriously become the body and blood of Christ

Trinity three ways of seeing God (Father, Son and Holy Spirit)

Vocation a special call from, or choosing by, God to do certain types of work

Whitsun the day when early Christians received the gift of the Holy Spirit. Also called Pentecost

NDEX